PIRATES AND PRIVA OUT OF BRISTOL

By

Ken Griffiths, Mark Steeds

and Roy Gallop

A History of Buccaneers and Sea Rovers

FIDUCIA PRESS

Fitting out the DUKE and DUCHESS in Bristol 1708 for Captain Woods Rogers Expedition.

— FRANK SHIPSIDES — 2004 —

PIRATES AND PRIVATEERS
OUT OF BRISTOL
A History of Buccaneers and Sea Rovers

By
Ken Griffiths and Mark Steeds

Foreword by Royston Alan Griffey
New Illustrations and Maps Roy Gallop
Book Design Roy Gallop and Ken Griffiths
Photographs and Graphic Editing Rosie Tomlinson
Typing Services Elaine Griffiths
Cover Illustrations Roy Gallop
Additional Photographs Carol Griffiths

FIDUCIA PRESS 2010
ISBN 978 0 946217 34 2
©Ken Griffiths and Mark Steeds
Printed in Great Britain by Doveton Press Ltd., Bristol.

CONTENTS

Front Cover. The pirate flag depicted is that used by the pirate 'Blackbeard'.
Title page. An impression of a !7th Century Buccaneer.
Page 2. 'The Duke' and the 'Duchess' at Bristol, preparing for Woodes Rogers' circumnavigation of the world.
A drawing by Bristol maritime artist Frank Shipsides. He was the first Patron of The Long John Silver Trust.
Page 3. A pirate brig running down a merchant galleass.
Back Cover : A sculpture of Woodes Rogers in Nassau.

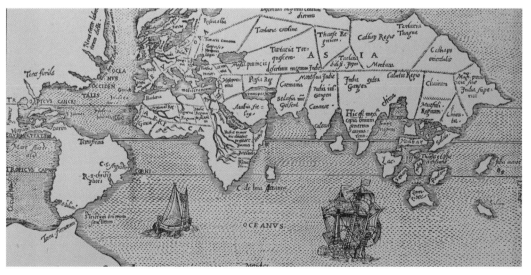

Thorne's woodcut showing the world in 1527, published by Hakluyt. Inaccurate maps, such as these, were all that the early adventurers had to guide them. Australia and New Zealand had not then been discovered.

The Ballad of the *Angel Gabriel*

This is a partisan account of the famous seventeenth century fight between Bristol seadogs in the privateer *Angel Gabriel* and three enemy ships during the Spanish war in the reign of Charles I. The story is told in a quaint anonymous ballad, of which the following is one version: -

The Honor of Bristol

Attend you, and give ear awhile, and you shall understand,
Of a battle fought upon the seas, by a ship of brave command:
The fight was so famous that all men's hearts did fill,
And make them cry "To sea with the *Angel Gabriel*."

The lusty ship of Bristol sailed out adventurously
Against the foes of England their strength with them to try:
Well victual'd, rig'd, and man'd, and good provision still,
Which made them cry "To sea with the *Angel Gabriel*."

The captain, famous Netheway, so he was called by name,
The master's name John Mines, a man of noted fame;
The gunner, Thomas Watson, a man of perfect skill,
With other valiant hearts in the *Angel Gabriel*.

They waving up and down the seas upon the ocean main,
"It is not long ago," quoth they, "since England fought with Spain";
Would we with them might meet, our minds for to fulfil,
We would play a noble bout with our *Angel Gabriel*."

They had no sooner spoken, than straight appeared in sight
Three lusty Spanish vessels, of warlike force and might;
With bloody resolution they thought our men to spill,
And vowed to make a prize of our *Angel Gabriel*.

Then first came up their Admiral, themselves for to advance –
In her she bore full forty-eight pieces of ordinance;
The next that came near us was their Vice-Admiral,
Which shot most furiously at our *Angel Gabriel*.

Our gallant ship had in her full forty fighting men,
With twenty pieces of ordinance we played about them then;
And with powder, shot and bullets, we did employ them still;
And thus began the fight with the *Angel Gabriel*.

Our captain to the master said, "Take courage, master bold;"
The master to the seamen said, "Stand fast, my hearts of gold;"
The gunner unto the rest, "Brave hearts be valiant

5

still;
Let us fight in the defence of our *Angel Gabriel*."

Then we gave them a broadside which shot their mast asunder,
And tore the boat-spret of their ship, which made the Spaniards wonder;
Which caused them to cry, with voices loud and shrill,
"Help, help, or else we sink, by the *Angel Gabriel*."

Yet desperately they boarded us, for all their valiant shot:
Three score of their best fighting men upon our decks we got;
And then at their first entrance full thirty did we kill,
And thus we cleared the decks of the *Angel Gabriel*.

With that their three ships boarded us again with might and main,
But still our noble Englishmen cried out, "A fig for Spain:"
Though seven times they boarded us, at last we showed our skill,
And made them feel the force of the *Angel Gabriel*.

Seven hours this fight continued, and many brave men lay dead,
With purple gore and Spanish blood the sea was coloured red;
Five hundred of their men we there outright did kill,
And many more were maim'd by the *Angel Gabriel*.

They seeing of these bloody spoils, the rest made haste away,
For why – they saw it was no boot any longer for to stay,
When they fled into to Cales, and there they must be still,
For they never more will dare to meet our *Angel Gabriel*.

We had within our English ship but only three men slain,
And five men hurt, the which I hope will soon be well again,
At Bristol we were landed, and let us praise God still,
That thus hath blessed our men, and our *Angel Gabriel*.

Now let us not forget to speak of the gift given by her owner
Of the *Angel Gabriel*, that many years have known her;
Two hundred pounds in coin and plate he gave with free good will,
Unto them that bravely fought in the *Angel Gabriel*.

FOREWORD

The romanticised picture of the pirate and buccaneer of centuries past conjures up that of a chivalrous *Robin Hood* of the High Seas nobly redistributing ill-gotten gains from the clutches of villainous adversaries for the benefit of the poor and down-trodden. Such deeds are naturally accomplished with the flourish of a feathered tri-corn, the flash of cold steel and a well aimed cannon shot over the bows of the opposing vessel ensuring the immediate and bloodless surrender of a heavily laden Spanish treasure ship. The picture is neatly rounded off with the immaculately attired Spanish captain gallantly releasing the beautiful daughter of the Governor of a British Colony in the Caribbean, who falls in love with the pirate chief.

This type of vision is so powerfully etched in the popular imagination, that one former Deputy Lord Mayor of Bristol suggested that all Bristolians were pirates at heart. No doubt he had in mind the adventurous, brave, courteous but somewhat foolhardy buccaneer who single-handedly wins through against all odds and returns home to a hero's welcome. Indeed, almost every child who steps aboard the famous Portuguese caravel, *The Matthew*, in Bristol's Floating Harbour immediately regards himself (or herself) to be a pirate, even though the replica medieval ship predates Caribbean buccaneering by several centuries. This same mysterious process often afflicts the accompanying parent as well, with accompanying cries of 'Argh! Jim lad!'

Unfortunately, the idealised portrayal of piracy and the pirate has little to do with reality. Just like the modern machine-gun toting marine gangsters operating in high-speed boats in and around the Horn of Africa, the principal aim of those piratical rogues of yesteryear was simply quick and easy profit. For anyone foolish enough to stand in their way or refuse to submit, then this singular purpose could be mixed with a deadly resolve of ruthlessness, violence and, in many cases, murder.

Probably, the most memorable pirate of popular fiction (ignoring some modern-day embodiments) is that of the infamous Long John Silver of the early film version of Robert Louis Stevenson's epic adventure story *Treasure Island*. The anti-hero, superbly depicted by Robert Newton as a somewhat loveable rogue with a heart of gold, is in truth a treacherous character quickly resorting to violence and murder in order to achieve his dubious ambitions. In fact, Silver represents an amalgam of some of the real life cut-throats who infested the Seven Seas with such nefarious intent as those represented in the pages that follow.

I think that this fascinating book, with so many Bristol connections, admirably separates fact from fiction and presents the pirate and buccaneer (and his predecessor the privateer) in a considerably less flattering light than the character of popular imagination. It also sheds light on many little known facets of piracy and the joint authors are to be commended for their labours. In conclusion, may I stray a little and briefly return to *The Matthew* story as another little known fact has also emerged through research by an

eminent historian at the University of Bristol, Dr Evan Jones. Following Cabot's voyages of discovery in 1497 and 1498, a previously unknown third expedition set off from Bristol in 1499 apparently led by the first Englishman to do so, William Weston, a man of Bristol. This has been revealed by a contemporary document that has recently come to light, and also provides the earliest recorded reference to *'The New Found Land'* of modern day Canada and America. It would seem that Master Weston of Bristol was a true adventurer and certainly not a pirate.

The Matthew in Bristol
City Docks

Royston Alan Griffey
Lord Mayor of Bristol in 2007/2008

Introduction

In the Fiducia Press publication of *Highway Robbery, a brief look at Highwaymen and Highwaywomen* I wrote that ….

It seems that highwaymen, in common with smugglers and pirates, will always be with us. With their rough edges smoothed out with the passing of time, they remain a source of inspiration to some and a source of romance to many, despite evidence to the contrary.

Whenever we think of pirates or buccaneers a mental picture is formed in our minds of seventeenth and eighteenth century figures cruising among the Caribbean Islands in search of plunder. They have become romantic figures because they no longer threaten us, unlike modern pirates who can still be a danger. In reality seventeenth and eighteenth century pirates, with very few exceptions, were renowned for their cruelty. This fact must be weighed against their achievement in navigation, skilled seamanship and the location of new lands.

The activities of the buccaneers became intertwined with the political ambitions of the newly emerging maritime powers, England, France and Holland. Buccaneers can be loosely defined as anyone who fought the Spanish, the common enemy who laid claim to vast territories in the New World and elsewhere. The Spanish of course considered any attack on their shipping or bases as piracy. Buccaneers engaged in an undeclared war on Spain, to which their respective governments turned a blind eye, chiefly because it was in their interests to do so.

Whenever war was declared on Spain the English, French or Dutch buccaneers became privateers, receiving authority from their governments to engage the Spanish wherever they found them. Later, when England, France and Holland turned on one another, as they did from time to time the buccaneers also operated as privateers, in effect being drafted into the navies of their respective governments.

The incursion into newly located lands by the European maritime powers is a sorry, sordid tale. They took over whole territories without the consent of the indigenous population and committed gross acts of cruelty while doing so. England, following the discovery of Haiti by the Spaniards in 1492 was content to use her sea-rovers to plunder bullion and other goods from Spanish ships or settlements. However, in the early seventeenth century England, together with France and Holland began to search for permanent bases that they could defend and from where they could extend their theatre of operations. Gradually, settlements or plantations were established and the defence of these became a priority.

The first joint settlement by the English and French governments took place in 1625 when a force of buccaneers invaded the West Indian island of St Christopher. They forced the Caribbee Indians off the islands after first killing their chiefs. This was a gross act of state piracy.

Incredibly, nearly 350 years after this land grab the British government carried out another act of state piracy when it forced out the entire population of an Indian Ocean island situated in the Chagos

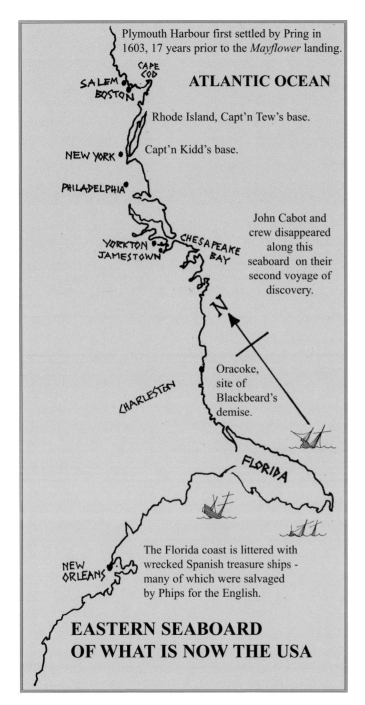

Plymouth Harbour first settled by Pring in 1603, 17 years prior to the *Mayflower* landing.

ATLANTIC OCEAN

Rhode Island, Capt'n Tew's base.

Capt'n Kidd's base.

John Cabot and crew disappeared along this seaboard on their second voyage of discovery.

Oracoke, site of Blackbeard's demise.

The Florida coast is littered with wrecked Spanish treasure ships - many of which were salvaged by Phips for the English.

EASTERN SEABOARD OF WHAT IS NOW THE USA

Archipelago. In 1961 an American naval officer, with the approval of the British government, put his heavy footprints of might over right onto Diego Garcia. This was the first step in the eventual use of this British colony as a US airbase. The islanders, who could trace their ancestry back for over 150 years, were transported without their consent to the island of Mauritius, a thousand miles distant. Imperialism dies hard it seems.

The invasion of St Christopher in 1625 was the start line in the gradual growth of British sea power. From haphazard beginnings the navy was eventually put under the single directing authority of the Admiralty in the mid seventeenth century. This major re-organization was the foundation of what became known as the Royal Navy. For good or ill the Royal Navy became a vital tool in the expansion of the British Empire.

Piracy has a long history; Julius Caesar was captured by pirates in 75BC whilst sailing to the Isle of Rhodes. Barbary Coast pirates were active during the same time as the European buccaneers were cruising the Caribbean. The Barbary Coast (the North African coastline between Morocco and Egypt) was notorious as a base for pirates between the sixteenth and eighteenth centuries. The Barbary pirates or corsairs as they were sometimes called, attacked shipping in the Mediterranean and even raided the shores of Britain. The newly organized English navy under Admiral Blake led an expedition into the Mediterranean and defeated the Barbary pirate fleet off Tunis in 1655 and secured the release of English captives destined for the slave markets. Piracy of course can be a recurring problem and currently there is an unwelcome revival of the practice (see Appendix 1).

The following narrative however will concern itself only with European involvement in piracy, in all its forms. Marks Steeds and I have divided this book into three parts. Part 1 will deal with the Spanish incursion into the Americas and the rise of the buc-caneers. Part 2 will cover the long distance voyages of privateers and the activities of some of the more infamous pirates. The book will conclude with the role of Bristol as a privateering centre in the period under discussion.

Ken Griffiths
Fiducia Press 2010

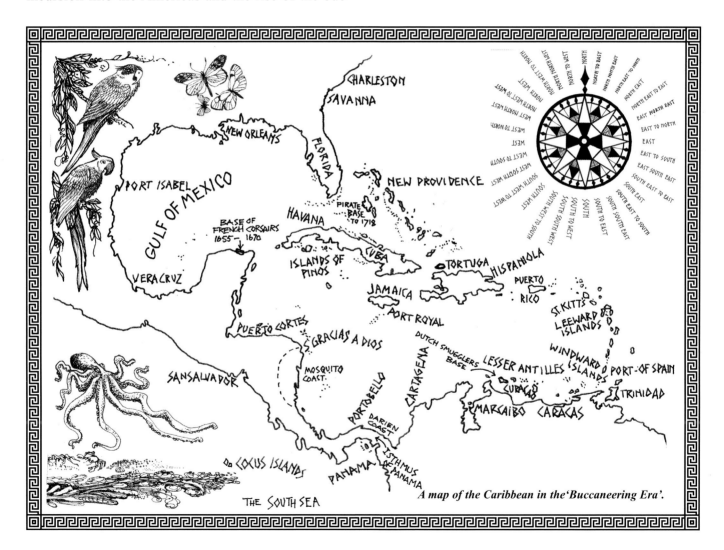

A map of the Caribbean in the 'Buccaneering Era'.

Part 1: The Coming of the Spanish and the Rise and Fall of the Buccaneers

The 'discovery' of the Caribbean by Columbus in 1492 started a chain reaction amongst the European maritime powers. Henry VII of England, having received intelligence of the existence of lands to the west, sent ships that led to the discovery of Newfoundland and other parts of North America.

The early English explorers did not, at first, lay claim to the lands they discovered, merely establishing trading posts. On the other hand Spain or to be more precise, Castile, on the merit of first discovery, claimed an exclusive right to the possession of the whole of America, with one exception; the Pope 'granted' Brazil to the Portuguese by means of a *Bull of Donation,* a papal legal document. This ruling by Pope Alexander VI was later challenged by the French and English buccaneers, often with the connivance of their respective governments.

Initially Spain considered the West Indies as the chief prize of all their possessions and it is not surprising that major hostilities took place in that region. Spain considered the New World as what we would call today 'treasure trove'. They believed they had a lawful right to take possession of the new lands, whether inhabited or not. A Royal Navy captain writing in 1816, could see the flaw in this argument. *(History of the Buccaneers of America' by* Captain James Burney, first published in 1816).

Nothing can be more opposed to common-sense, than that strangers should pretend to acquire by discovery a title to countries they find with inhabitants; as if in those very inhabitants the right of prior discovery was not inherent.

This is a charge that could also be laid against the British government in the establishment of its own Empire.

English and French ships visited South America very early, refusing to accept the papal ruling. At first the Spanish were left to occupy and administer their island colonies unmolested by the other European maritime powers. But this 'hands off' policy was not to last.

The first colony established by Spain in their newly discovered world was on the island known to the native inhabitants as Haiti or Hayti*. The Spaniards however named their new possession Española or Hispaniola. The Spanish found the people gentle and compassionate and therefore easy prey. Queen Isabella, who was the patroness of Columbus also became patroness of the discovery and believed that she was duty bound to protect the native population, providing of course that they accepted the presence of her countrymen. Hispaniola however was rich in gold and the rights of the people were soon overlooked as the need for mine labour became a priority for the invader.

First meetings between Columbus and the native population passed without incident. Indeed, the crew of one of his ships wrecked off the coast had every reason to be grateful to the local inhabitants.

* In this narrative the word Hispaniola will be used as this was the name marked on maps of the period.

Replica of the late 15th century 'Matthew'. Crewed by Bristol seamen the original ship reached Newfoundland in 1497.

that encouraged the court of Spain to give Columbus such a wide range of authority in the New World. To quote James Burney again ….

This was the first step in the iniquitous usurpations which the more cultivated nations of the world have practiced upon their weaker brethren.

On his return to Hispaniola Columbus found the fortified stockade demolished and the garrison destroyed. It appeared that the rapacity and licentious conduct of the garrison had provoked even the naturally peaceful islanders into a violent reaction. Betrayal and an understandable violent reaction was eventually to become the pattern in all the Americas. Another fort was built and more Spanish arrived. The islanders then came to an understanding that the intention of the newcomers was to stay. The visitors had become invaders and occupiers.

Various strategies were employed by the islanders to rid themselves of their uninvited guests. The local population no longer delivered supplies to the town and garrison, a peaceful response to the problem. This only encouraged the Spaniards to take provisions by force and this increased resentment amongst the islanders. Although the atrocities committed against the native population were excused by the early Spanish settlers because they were in fear of their lives, the reverse is true. The islanders were always amenable to negotiation even in the worst of times. Columbus knew that a sufficiently strong force could subdue Hispaniola, but it would be more prudent to find other ways to bring the native population to a state of subservience. A chieftain named

They used every means available to effect a rescue and offered care to the exhausted crew members. When Columbus returned to Europe he left behind a small garrison housed in a fortified stockade. A number of islanders volunteered to accompany Columbus to Spain. He also took gold and samples of native craft work. It was probably the presence of gold in Hispaniola and its association with power

Coanabo was approached and terms offered that seemed so reasonable that he agreed to them. With complete trust and relying on the good faith of the Spaniards he put himself in a situation that led to his capture. He was taken on board a ship bound for Spain, but it foundered during the voyage. It was the first in a long line of broken treaties spread over many centuries.

The islanders were outraged at this betrayal and rose up in a defensive war. Columbus responded by fielding a force armed with muskets and cross-bows. He also had at his disposal a troop of cavalry and twenty large dogs. These dogs were not used for tracking only, but for attack. It was not possible for the islanders to withstand such a ferocious onslaught. The numbers employed by Columbus were in truth small, but they had a discipline the islanders lacked. The dogs particularly filled the islanders with dread. Many of the natives were savaged to death by the dogs. Islanders who tried to escape from the soldiers were pursued by the dogs and their handlers. There was no mercy shown during this manhunt. Columbus wanted a complete victory to terrorize the population into submission. Such a way of waging war was outside the scope of the islanders' experience. Thousands were killed and those taken prisoner were made slaves. Three hundred islanders were taken to Spain as slaves. After Columbus' victory it is estimated that a third of the native population died of famine and by suicide in a few months. For the next nine months Columbus marched across Hispaniola exacting fines or demanding tribute of gold and cotton.

Queen Isabella was appalled at Columbus' actions. She returned the captured slaves to Hispaniola and issued instructions that none of the islanders should be enslaved. The colonists however, using Columbus as their example, ignored this instruction. Many of the islanders were forced to work in the gold mines, at first for a small wage (probably to pay lip service to Queen Isabella's instruction), but the pretence that they were adequately rewarded for forced work was soon abandoned and they became forced labourers without pay, in fact slaves.

In 1500 Columbus was replaced as governor-general by Francisco de Boradilla, with new instructions that all slaves should be freed. Boradilla also ignored this order and continued to use slaves in the gold mines. He in turn was replaced by Don Nicolas Orando who at first followed orders that the slaves should be freed. Probably because the output of gold decreased Orando forcibly returned the islanders to the mines, some forced to live as well as work underground. They were literally worked to death and there was such a shortage of labour that slaves were imported from Africa. The Africans however stiffened resistance to the occupation and uprisings became more common.

The colonization of Hispaniola revealed the contradictory nature of Queen Isabella's character. Anxious to be seen as the protectress of the native population she nonetheless gave enormous authority to Columbus stating that ….

Attack dogs were not only used by the Spanish as this 17th century engraving of English seamen illustrates. The dog depicted is a Bristol Mastiff on Pring's expedition.

A match ignition musket.

Forasmuch, as you, Christopher Columbus, are going by our command, with our vessels and our men to discover and subdue certain islands and continent our will is, that you shall be our admiral, viceroy and governor in them.

No room here for the mere establishing of trading posts with the consent of the local population. It is a pointless exercise to issue instructions against slave labour when you have given authority for whole peoples to be subdued. Local administrators and military men often became tyrants using this early instruction as an excuse for barbarity and personal gain. By 1511, Cuba, the largest of the Caribbean islands, was invaded by the Spanish. The inhabitants were terrorized by Spanish soldiery into submitting in less than a year. There were several attempts in the sixteenth century by Dominican friars to at least improve the conditions of native populations. Cardinal Ximeres, on becoming prime minister of Spain sent Bartolomeo de Las Casas to Hispaniola with the title of *Protector of the Indians*. But all the efforts of Las Casas and the Dominicans were of no avail and the scene was set for the wholesale involvement of Spaniards into the lives of the indigenous population of North, Central and South America; betrayals, massacres and dispossessions. Sadly, the colonization of Hispaniola became the model for other European powers in their drive for Empires throughout the World.

The Dominican Las Casas worked for many years in the Americas. He saw at first hand the exploitation of native populations and listened with increasing horror to the settlers justification for their barbarities. Las Casas believed that the most effective way to influence people was by humility and good example. In his own words ….

No nation that exists, no matter how rude, uncivilized and barbarous, savage or brutal, cannot be persuaded into a good way of life - provided that the method used is that proper and natural to men - namely love, gentleness and kindness.

Las Casas' aim was not only to free slaves from bondage but to stop all Spanish conquests of America. At last, at the age of seventy-six he got his chance. In 1550 Charles V of Spain suspended all further conquests until the matter was debated. Juan Gines de Sepulveda, a philosopher, who had never been to the New World, put his case to Charles V's advisers, the *Council of Fourteen*. Basically he approved of further conquests as it was in Spain's interests to do so. The views of the indigenous population of the New World should not be taken into account as they were uncivilized and therefore barely human, perhaps not human at all. There was therefore no need to attempt the conversion of the native population. Sepulveda was giving the green light to continued exploitation of millions of people.

Las Casas could put his case before the *Council of Fourteen* armed with facts and figures based on personal experience and it is not surprising that he won the debate. The following is part of his testament.

For all the peoples of the world are human beings. And the definition of humans, collectively and severally, is one: that they are rational beings. All possess understanding and volition, being formed in the image and likeness of God; all have the natural capacity or faculties to understand and master the knowledge that they do not have - all take pleasure in goodness and all abhor evil. All men are alike in what concerns their creation. And no one is born enlightened. From this it follows that all of us must be guided and aided at first by those who were born before us. And the savage peoples of the earth may be compared to uncultivated soil that readily brings forth weeds and useless thorns, but has within itself such natural virtue that by labour and cultivation it may be made to yield sound and beneficial fruits. Thus all humankind is one.

This was a declaration of human rights over human greed and a warning against the demonisation of people we fear or do not understand.

Although Las Casas won the debate, vested interests won the day, as they do in our own times and conquests were resumed. Currently, great efforts are being made to encourage governments of powerful nations to adopt ethical foreign policies, but as we have seen these are often breached 'in the national interest'. It was in the 'national interest' of Spain that the conquests should continue, with resultant wars, exploitation and theft of land, not just by Spain but by other European maritime powers. Human rights are still under siege today and it would be as

Bartolomeo de Las Casas addressing the 'Council of Fourteen'

well to remember what transpired after 'the great debate' of 1550 when 'the national interest' became more important than *love, gentleness and kindness. .*

As we have seen Spain considered they had exclusive rights over the Spanish Indies and would con-

sider any infringement as an act of piracy. In 1517 or perhaps 1518 news reached Spain that an English ship had been sighted in the West Indies. This caused much alarm to the authorities. The circumstances were these.

A caravel (a sailing ship of Mediterranean design) sailing from the principal Spanish port in Hispaniola, San Domingo, on its way to Puerto Rico sighted a ship of some 250 tons. The ship was well armed with cannon. A boat was sent from the caravel to ascertain the ship's destination. There was surprise when the commander explained that he and his crew were English. This caused much consternation amongst the Spaniards, an English ship in the Spanish Indies, a territory in which they believed they had exclusive rights. The Spaniards were even more perturbed when the commander of the English vessel revealed that they had already been to Puerto Rico after first visiting Brazil. The English ship's next landfall was San Domingo itself and a request made to sell their goods to the settlers. This was a bold (or naïve) move and the response was swift. The governor ordered the fort to open fire on the ship which forced it to leave. According to the *Historia General de las Indias* by Hernandez de Oviedo the English vessel then returned to Puerto Rico and traded provisions for the wrought iron she was carrying. This voyage by a single ship (although the commander explained to the crew of the caravel that he had been separated from another ship in a storm), was obviously well planned and financed. Armed and adequately filled with trade goods this vessel had sailed with a purpose. The fact that they could find their way to Brazil, Puerto Rico and Hispaniola indicated that they knew more than they revealed to the crew of the caravel. Much of their intelligence probably came from the French who were also roaming the seas at this time. This sharing of information became well established among the French and English buccaneers in later years.

Although the English vessel was repulsed by force at San Domingo the crew found no such hostility from the Spanish settlers in Puerto Rico. Away from the prying eyes of the Spanish administrators they were able to trade under more favourable terms with the English. The Spanish Court's monopoly had been broken. Illicit trading was eventually to spread to Hispaniola itself, but only in the isolated settlements. Incursions into the Spanish Indies by English, French and Dutch vessels became more frequent and although their sails were not a common sight, the Spaniards felt their presence, the lull before the storm.

The unnamed English ship that had caused such a stir in the Spanish Court was almost certainly from Bristol, crewed by adventurers. Although capable of defending themselves they were first and foremost traders, with no interest in conquest or settlement. There has been a long tradition of Bristolians fishing for cod off the Grand Banks of Newfoundland, some years before John Cabot's voyage in the *Matthew* in 1497. It was probably no accident that Cabot chose to sail from Bristol where skilled transatlantic seamen congregated. There is a similar tradition amongst the Bretons and the Basques. The knowledge gained from these voyages was not universally shared, except of course with other seamen. Perhaps

Columbus did not sail completely 'into the unknown'. Denied trading facilities by force, except for small scale illicit transactions, the European freebooters began to attack Spanish ships. At first this activity was sporadic and undertaken mostly by the French. These attacks however were considered such a threat that the Spanish authorities tried to establish a convoy system for their ships. Under this

A sculpture of a late 15th century Bristol seaman situated in the city docks; a representatation of John Cabot.

scheme ships would rendezvous at a port in Hispaniola and sail together for mutual support. The plan was approved by the *Council of the Indies,* but, for reasons unknown, never implemented. This was a big mistake as it made attacks by filibusters* and freebooters more likely. When these seamen began to co-operate with each other, whatever their nationality, attacks on Spanish ships became more frequent.

*From the French flibustier.

17

As Spain concentrated on the conquest of mainland America her resources were transferred to that region. The Spanish Indies became less important to the Spanish government in Spain and the settlers were expected to be resourceful in the management of their colonies. Due to the shortage of labour some of the mines on the islands were no longer in operation. The settlers in Hispaniola, experiencing the same problem began to diversify into sugar-cane cultivation. They also engaged in cattle hunting which turned out to be very profitable. The Spaniards named their hunters *matadores* which translates into *killers* or *slaughterers*.

A new threat was also looming for the Spanish at about this time. The English, French and Dutch began to make some inroads into Hispaniola. There were huge stretches of coast, with good bays for ships on the west coast and largely uninhabited by the native population. It was fat with cattle and also had the advantage of being of considerable distance from the Spanish capital of San Domingo. In bays and inlets the European seamen could re-provision their ships in security. An added bonus was the willingness of Spanish settlers to trade with them. They were only too keen to secure European goods on less exorbitant terms than that demanded by agents of the Royal Monopoly. The Spanish government at San Domingo tried to stop this practice by allocating ships to clear the coast of these European seamen, an operation not without its risks. In response the English, French and Dutch freebooters organised themselves into a loose confederation, calling themselves 'Brethren of the Coast'. They felt secure enough to set up factories in Hispaniola to skin cattle and to cure the flesh, using these items as a product of trade. In all this they had the clandestine support of their respective governments. Of course, if caught by the Spanish they were 'on their own' and could expect no help, their governments denying any responsibility for the actions of these early buccaneers.

This undeclared war on Spain by the other maritime powers of Europe performed various functions, the chief of which was to limit the power of Spain. As the sixteenth century advanced the adventurers, filibusters and freebooters became a force to be reckoned with. The massive support given by Elizabeth I of England to her piratical or privateering seamen emboldened them to undertake aggressive expeditions. In 1586 Francis Drake plundered San Domingo itself. This increasing activity of English and French seamen in the West Indies led to the abandonment of all the western and north western parts of Hispaniola by the Spanish.

The increasing trade of the English and French freebooters in the West Indies demanded bases they could work from. From tentative footholds in Hispaniola they gradually began to colonise territory in other islands. The intention from the start was that these settlements would be permanent. These moves by the adventurers and freebooters was welcomed by their respective governments. As these rover seamen were still weak compared to the power of Spain it was suggested that both the English and French freebooters should jointly administer one island for mutual support.

The island thought to be the best for this joint venture was St Christopher (St Kitts), one of the Small Antilles or Caribbee Islands. This was the first of the West Indian islands to be seized by the early buccaneers with colonization in mind. What was also notable was that they were used to enforce their respective governments' foreign policies, a pattern that was to become familiar throughout the seventeenth century.

In 1625 a party of English and French freebooters landed on St Christopher and took possession of the island in the name of their respective governments. St Christopher was inhabited by Caribbee Indians

This replica of the 'Golden Hind' was typical of the ocean going vessels operating out of Bristol in the 16th century.

and although the Spanish had no settlements on the island they often called there to trade for provisions. They did however consider they had exclusive rights over the island due to the *Bull of Donation,* whether they had a settlement there or not.

The English and French took possession of the island without the consent of the native Caribbs. Naturally there was resentment by the native population. Using as an excuse that they were allied to the Spanish the invaders made a surprise night attack on the local population. Their chiefs were killed and the people forced to flee the island. As James Burney states ….

Thus in usurpation and barbarity was founded the first colony established under the authority of the British and French governments in the West Indies; which colony was the parent of our African slave trade.

There was an earlier attempt by the English to establish a slave trade, but it was of short duration. In 1562 John Hawkyns raided the Barbary Coast and the west coast of Africa and kidnapped hundreds of Africans. His fleet sailed to the Americas and the slaves, who had endured unspeakable horrors during the voyage, were sold to Spanish settlers. Hawkyns, with the full backing of Elizabeth 1 of England, undertook two more slaving voyages. The final expedition ended in disaster when the English were defeated in a fleet action with the Spanish off the coast of Mexico in September 1568. The *Judith,* commanded by Francis Drake and the *Minion,* Hawkyns' ship, managed to escape from the battle and made their way home independently. Hawkyns, short of stores, abandoned 114 of his men on the Mexican coast.

Tension soon developed between the English and French. When the English settlers took over the neighbouring island of Nevis in 1629 matters came to a head. The Spanish were at war with England, France and Holland at the time and the Spanish and French had large fleets in the area. A squadron of French king's ships arrived and by taking several English ships forced the English governor to comply with the original agreement. The French squadron then left St Christopher, but no sooner than they were out of sight of the island a strong fleet of thirty-nine Spanish ships appeared on the horizon. The Spanish easily took over the island. Some of the French escaped in their ships and took refuge among islands to the north. Those left, together with the English were taken prisoners of war. It was fortunate that a state of war existed between Spain and the other European maritime powers, as the treatment the settlers would have received may have been rather different. The commander of the Spanish fleet, Don Frederic de Toledo, took as many of the prisoners as he could aboard his own ships, but others he allowed to use any vessels they had to leave the island. As there were insufficient craft to take all the settlers many had to stay. Don Frederic demanded their parole that they would leave the island as soon as vessels called for them. He issued a threat to those he had allowed to leave the island and to those he had allowed to temporarily stay. The threat was stark; he said that if, on his return from Brazil he found any Englishmen or Frenchmen on St Christopher he would put them to the sword.

The Spanish fleet then left for Brazil, Don Frederic satisfied that he had resolved the problem of the interlopers. This action displayed the power of Spain, but it also revealed its weakness. Don Frederic could not secure St Christopher with men on the ground. Spain was in fact over extended and the colonists knew that Spain would always give priority to home defence and to its possessions on the mainland and consequently the English and French soon returned to St Christopher. The presence of colonists on St Christopher made the hunters on the west coast of Hispaniola feel more secure. Their factories for the curing of meat and for the drying of skins increased in number. The French settlers on Hispaniola (for in reality this is what the hunters had become) took possession of the small island of Tortuga as a place of refuge from any major attack from the Spanish. Tortuga was well stocked with goods and military equipment for defence. There was however no command structure for the defence of the island, a flaw that was later to have devastating consequences.

It was about this time that the hunters began to be known as buccaneers. At first it only referred to the hunters based in Hispaniola, but was later to become a generic word to describe any European sea-rovers who fought the Spanish. It largely replaced the words adventurers, filibusters and freebooters. The word filibuster was merely the French mariner's way of pronouncing the English word freebooters. The word buccaneer probably came from the way hunters cured the flesh of cattle in order that it would keep over long periods, the technique having been learnt from the Caribbee Indians. The method involved placing the meat on a wooden grate (which the Indians called a *barbecu*), sited at a good distance over a slow burning fire. When the meat was cured it was called *boucan* and the curers of meat called *boucaniers*. English buccaneers called themselves *privateers* when commissioned by their government to act for them in time of war. The instrument of this commission was a *Letter of Marque*.

By about 1630 Spain realised that it could no longer claim or hold all of the West Indies. They became less aggressive with their claims in the hope that their long established island settlements would be spared from attack. This was only partially successful as we shall see.

The number of settlers on Tortuga grew; they cultivated the land and planted tobacco, which proved to be of good quality. Many Europeans set up colonies on some of the islands of the Small Antilles with the support of the buccaneers. The vast majority of these settlers were English and French, but the Dutch also had a presence. Their governments became interested in these ventures and began to grant land tenures to favoured individuals at home once the buccaneers and settlers had secured the new colonies. Many of the first settlers were displaced and this caused much resentment. This casual disregard for the people who had cleared and cultivated the land led to large numbers of settlers joining the buccaneers. It should be noted that the first settlers also had a casual disregard for the native population. There is no doubt that an injustice was perpetrated by the home governments against the first settlers and buccaneers, but the parent of this injustice was the invasion and occupation of what we would call today *sovereign states*.

Although the buccaneers were becoming more powerful they could not at this time withstand a major assault by the Spanish, particularly if the settlers were occupying a small island. Spain would always react if they thought its strategic situation was in peril. Tortuga had long been a thorn in the Spaniards' side and in 1636 they launched a skilful attack on the island. Probably acting on intelligence they made their move when a large number of settlers were hunting cattle on the western part of Hispaniola. There was no commander in Tortuga to organize an effective defence and the Spaniards met little resistance. All settlers who fell into their hands were killed and even those that came from their hiding places to surrender were hanged. A few of the settlers managed to escape to join their brethren in Hispaniola.

The Spanish hoped they had taught the settlers a lesson by the harsh treatment they had inflicted on them. It is likely that they had allowed a few settlers to escape so the news of the massacre could be spread far and wide, as a warning not to return to Tortuga. The Spanish did not garrison the island, being content to destroy the buildings and burn the plantations, a practice brought into modern times. The Spaniards left and returned to San Domingo.

To make Tortuga really secure they first had to deal with the buccaneers on Hispaniola and this they failed to do, probably because to do so would be expensive both in men and money. The hope that there would be no return of the settlers to Tortuga proved to be just wishful thinking. The massacre of the settlers on Tortuga had instilled in the survivors not fear but revenge. Ably helped by the buccaneers they once again occupied Tortuga. This time a commander was appointed and the defences of the island strengthened. The Spanish attack on Tortuga had the effect of uniting the English, French and Dutch buccaneers into an even closer liaison against the common enemy.

As usual the involvement of home governments in the affairs of the buccaneers and settlers stimulated old rivalries. France took formal possession of Tortuga in 1645, and forced out the English buccaneers. The French heavily fortified Western Hispaniola, ostensibly to protect them from the Spanish, but had the effect of depriving the English buccaneers of bases and boucan. In future the English would have to find their own bases. When buccaneers operated independently of their respective governments co-operation between the English and French continued as before. The buccaneers were still needed by governments as periodically they required a well-trained and experienced military force they could rely on.

In 1654 a large force of English and French buccaneers mounted an expedition on a part of the American mainland called the Mosquito Coast. They voyaged in canoes up a river on the south side of Cape Gracias a Dios. It was a most hazardous journey, the buccaneers having to contend with waterfalls and a very strong stream. They eventually left their canoes and marched to the town of Nueva Segoria. The buccaneers plundered this town and returned downstream to the coast. This expedition was a bold move by the buccaneers and it had the effect of making the Spaniards feel that few places were safe from attack. They responded by taking Tortuga from the French and this time they left a garrison on the island.

In 1655 England was at war with Spain again and a large fleet sent from England. The English attacked Hispaniola with the aim of taking it from the Spanish. This was not a raid for plunder, they had settlement in mind. However they were thwarted by a vigorous defence and the fleet moved on to Jamaica which they took and held. This was an important strategic position, being halfway between Cuba and Hispaniola. Buccaneers were used to assist the English forces in the conquest of this island, their local knowledge being of paramount importance. Buccaneers were active again a few years later when they assisted in the re-taking of Tortuga from Spain. Fleets were sent from Spain but they were unable to expel the French from Hispaniola or Tortuga. The buccaneers, with their vast local knowledge and skilled seamanship, were an important ancillary force at the disposal of the English and French governments.

As the activities of the buccaneers became more audacious and widespread their leaders or captains became more well known. Stories abounded concerning their daring deeds but they were chiefly known for their notoriety. Pierre Le Grand, a

Frenchman from Dieppe, in a small boat with a crew of just twenty eight men, captured a Spanish galleon laden with treasure and other goods. He set down the crew of the galleon on western Hispaniola and then proceeded to sail his prize to France. Another Frenchman, Alexandre, took on a Spanish man-of-war and against all odds captured the vessel. Yet another Frenchman, Montbars, had such a ferocious reputation that he was named the *Exterminator*. A Portuguese buccaneer named Bartolomeo Portuguez was renowned for his escapes from battles and the gallows.

One of the most feared buccaneers was known as Francois l'Olonnois, although it was doubtful if this was the Frenchman's real name. Together with another buccaneer commander, Michel le Busque, they led a force of over six hundred men and took the towns of Maracaibo and Gibraltar in the Gulf of Venezuela. They seized plunder valued at 400,000 crowns. Many atrocities were committed during the action. L'Olonnois was determined to make sure that his enemies knew he would show them no mercy. Many stories have been recounted about l'Olonnois' cruelty, including the execution of the entire crew of a Spanish ship, ninety men in all. It is also said that he had the crews of four ships tossed into the sea, but one of the most grisly tales has it that he ripped the hearts out of some of his victims and ate them. These stories of course may have been exaggerations, or been concocted and spread by l'Olonnois himself to enhance his reputation as a merciless antagonist. A fearful reputation could be used as a terror weapon and Blackbeard certainly used this ploy some years later. Whatever the truth

of these tales there is little room for doubt that Francois l'Olonnois did commit acts of gross barbarity. Surrounding himself with so much violence it is not surprising that he died a violent death. He met his end at the hand of Indians on the Darien coast.

The buccaneers were now so feared that some Spanish settlements, both on the American mainland and on the West Indian islands, began to pay protection money. Henry Morgan, an English buccaneer teamed up with a man of unknown nationality called Monsvelt. On Monsvelt's death Morgan took over a leadership role amongst the buccaneers. Henry Morgan (1635-1688) was born in South Wales. There are accounts that he was kidnapped as a young man in Bristol and transported to Barbados. There is however a record of him being indentured but this may have been a device to give a doubtful legality to the process. Whatever the truth of the matter there does seem to have been some instances of children being kidnapped to work in the plantations during the mid seventeenth century. The passing of an ordinance in 1654 by the Bristol Corporation to prohibit the kidnapping and transportation of 'boys, maids and others' must have been a response to public concern. How this ordinance was administered was examined by the author Derek Robinson in 1973.*

Henry Morgan led many raids against the Spanish and Dutch in the West Indies and Central America. His most notable raid was on Panama in defiance of the *Treaty of America* between England and Spain (see Appendix 2). To placate the Spanish he was arrested, but was eventually knighted when hostilities were resumed with Spain. It can be seen that the

*See *A Shocking History of Bristol*
by Derek Robinson.

English government did not take treaties seriously as there were many advantages to be gained by clandestinely supporting the free roving buccaneers. Morgan returned to Jamaica and became deputy-governor of that island. Henry Morgan's activities and atrocities will be discussed in more detail in Part 2 of this book.

In 1680 a force of some three hundred buccaneers crossed the Isthmus of Panama to what was then known as The South Sea (Pacific Ocean). They captured Spanish ships and used these to further their aims of plunder. In this they were ably assisted by the Darien Indians, with whom the English had good relations. Perhaps the most valuable commodity and certainly the most useful to new generations of seamen was the seizure of Spanish charts from a captured vessel. These were taken to England and put to good use by the government. The buccaneers of this South Sea expedition began to dispute whether they should return across the isthmus or continue their voyages. In democratic fashion they voted for their preference. The party that secured the highest number of votes would keep the ship and the others be given the long boat and canoes and return to the West Indies across the isthmus. Captain Bartholomew Sharp's party polled the highest number of votes and kept the ship, which was eventually to return to the West Indies the long way round, i.e. via the tip of South America. At the time of these events England was not at war with Spain and demands were made that the buccaneers be treated as pirates. There were show trials of course but in general the buccaneers got away with it. The English government had secured good charts of the west coast of South America and was now well aware that the Spanish no longer felt safe in formerly secure areas.

Soon after the circumnavigation of South America by Captain Sharp and his men William Dampier began to venture into the South Sea. Dampier had been a member of the 1680 expedition but was one of the party that elected to return to the West Indies via the isthmus. William Dampier (1652-1715) was born in the Somerset village of East Coker. He was

renowned for his navigational skills. After journeys to Newfoundland and the West Indies he became a member of the buccaneer gang that crossed the isthmus in 1680. From 1683 he crossed the Pacific to the Philippines, China and Australia. He published his *New Voyage round the World* in 1697. In 1699 he led a voyage of discovery to the South Seas mapping the North West coast of Australia, then known as New Holland. He gave his name to the 'Dampier Archipelago' and 'Dampier Strait' and made two more significant voyages in the very early part of the eighteenth century. William Dampier will be studied in greater depth in Part 2 of this book.

From 1683 the buccaneers became more numerous on the western coast of South America. Treasure ships were consistently under threat and reinforcements were sent from Spain. This was necessary as the buccaneers were quite capable of combining forces to fight fleet actions. On one occasion the Viceroy of Peru gathered together a fleet to protect the transport of treasure to Panama (for transport across the isthmus to waiting ships bound for Spain). Even so the commander of the Spanish fleet was ordered to avoid action until the treasure had been landed. By sailing an indirect course the Spanish fleet managed to reach Panama undetected. The treasure was unloaded and the fleet went in search of the buccaneers. Eventually the two fleets came in sight of one another. The buccaneer fleet could muster ten vessels with a total of 960 men. With the exception of two ships, the *Cygnet* and the *Batchelor's Delight* none of the buccaneers ships had cannon. Captain Edward Davis of the *Batchelor's Delight* was considered to be the Admiral. His ship

carried thirty six guns. The *Cygnet*, commanded by Captain Swan carried sixteen cannon. However, the lack of cannon in the other ships was not considered a drawback; the buccaneers had an ample supply of small arms and were well skilled in their use. The buccaneers were close quarter fighters and their tactics were to board an enemy vessel at the first opportunity. The Spanish fleet had fourteen ships of which six were fitted with cannon. As the Spaniards were superior in cannon and the buccaneers superior in musketry it was to the advantage of the Spaniards that they engaged in distance fighting. The buccaneers intention was to board and to this end Davis bore down on the Spanish fleet. This was a bold move and stood a good chance of success but Davis was admiral in name only and the independence and indiscipline of the buccaneers led to the break-up of

the attack. With the exception of an exchange of cannon fire between Davis's ship and the ship of the Spanish vice-admiral the fleets failed to engage. If

Davis and 'his' buccaneers had secured a victory they would have had virtual control of the South Sea.

However, Davis did distinguish himself in another action. The town of Guayaquil had been taken by a combined force of English and French buccaneers. On receiving intelligence that two large Spanish men-of-war were on their way to retake the town Davis sailed to intercept them. This interception was vital to the buccaneers on Guayaquil as the presence of the warships would prevent them escaping with their plunder. Davis could only call on two small ships to assist him in the engagement. The battle spread over several days and took the form of distance firing, each side manoeuvring for a wind favourable to them. The Spanish realised that only by getting up close could they bring matters to a conclusion. This they were not prepared to do, despite the odds being very much in their favour, the Spanish being well aware of the buccaneers skill in musketry and ferocity in close quarter fighting. The engagement ended when the Spaniards withdrew. The Spanish should have had another cannon armed warship with them at the time of the engagement with Davis, the *Katalina*. This ship had earlier become separated from the main force and had the misfortune to run into the *Batchelor's Delight*. Davis immediately fell upon the Spanish ship and after a sharp action the *Katalina* was driven on shore where she beached. The English and French buccaneers gave Davis and his crew a share of the booty they had amassed in Guayaquil in recognition of their assistance.

Davis and his crew sailed to the Galapagos Islands to careen* their ship and re-provision. They stocked up with cured fish and salted land turtle. They extracted gallons of oil from the land turtles which was considered by the seamen as a delicacy and used it as a butter substitute. Davis took leave of the Galapagos and set course for Cape Horn. On the way to the Horn the *Batchelor's Delight* survived a sea-quake and the account by Davis of its effects is one of the first recorded in that part of the world.

Davis and his crew eventually came across a previously undiscovered island. Davis, although he made no landing gave a sufficiently good description for us to be able to identify it as Easter Island. The buccaneers made landfall in the West Indies in 1688 being well aware that their recent activities could be considered piracy. Their only defence was that they only took up arms against the Spanish and did not attack English or French ships. The English government particularly was anxious to come to an accommodation with the Spanish and saw the activities or even the presence of buccaneers as an obstacle to

Cleaning the underside of the hull.

this progress. There was much resentment, even outrage amongst the buccaneers at the double standards displayed by the government. Over the years the government had shamefully and shamelessly used the buccaneers to enforce its foreign policy and ambitions, at little cost or physical risk to its members. Having encouraged, if not creating the monster, the government was trying to return it to the cage. Hypocritically the government called on the buccaneers in time of war to act as privateers as it was cheaper than keeping a large standing fleet in need of constant training. This attitude was to sow the seed that later grew into widespread piracy when ships of all nations were subject to attack and required much effort and cost to suppress.

Davis was fortunate that he had arrived in the West Indies at a time when the king's pardon was offered to all buccaneers that gave up their way of life. All the crew, including Davis, took the pardon, a secure and satisfying end to their long and arduous voyage.

James Burney gives his account of their good fortune and with it his testament to Edward Davis ….

It was not the least of fortune's favours to this crew of buccaneers that they should find it in their power, without any care or forethought of their own, to terminate a long course of piratical adventures in quietness and security. Edward Davis was afterwards in England, as appears by the notice given of his discovery by William Dampier, who mentions him always with peculiar respect. Though a buccaneer, he was a man of much sterling worth, being an excellent commander, courageous, never rash, and

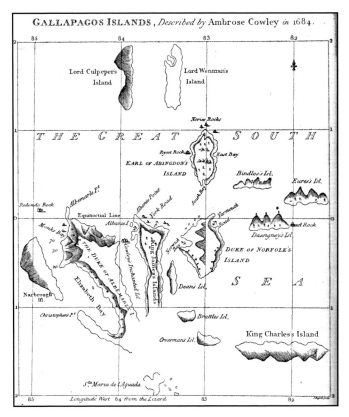

endued in a superior degree with prudence, moderation, and steadiness, qualities in which the buccaneers generally have been most deficient. His character is not stained with acts of cruelty; on the contrary, wherever he commanded, he restrained the ferocity of his companions. It is no small testimony to his abilities that the whole of the buccaneers in the South Sea during this time, in every enterprise wherein he bore part, voluntarily placed themselves under his guidance, and paid him obedience as their leader; and no symptom occurs of their having at any time wavered in this respect or shown inclination to set up a rival authority. It may also be said that the only matter in which they were not capri-

cious was their confidence in his management; and in it they found their advantage, if not their preservation.

Other buccaneers made long voyages with an eye to the main chance, i.e. the collection of booty. They did however make various discoveries and greatly added to the knowledge of the world. Not interested in settlement or the acquisition of new territory they were generous in their sharing of their growing understanding of new lands. After the battle in the Bay of Panama the *Cygnet* commanded by Captain Swan commenced a voyage that would take her from the South Sea on the west coast of Central America to the East Indies, Philippines and New Holland (the west coast of Australia). The *Cygnet* only ended her voyage when she foundered off the coast of Madagascar. During the voyage the crew had deposed Captain Swan in a bloodless mutiny, abandoning him and thirty six others on the island of Mindanao. Dampier had remained with the crew on the ship, but subsequently denied being involved in the mutiny. He elected to leave the *Cygnet* at the Nicobar Islands, near Sumatra, probably because of her unseaworthy condition. He returned to England in 1691. Some of the crew stranded in Madagascar made their way home in European ships that regularly, if infrequently, called at the island.

These voyages by the buccaneers were risky ventures in terms of their personal safety. They often sailed in uncharted seas and had problems in fixing longitude. It would be another hundred years before this particular problem was solved. The buccaneers would be uncertain as to what sort of reception they would receive from the native populations and of course there was also the danger of the Spanish presence. The Dutch already had settlements in the East Indies and could become at least suspicious of English interlopers. There was a danger of shipwreck on uninhabited islands way off the trade routes which would give the buccaneers little chance of rescue. They were also at risk by the very nature of their trade; the buccaneers were first and foremost plunderers and would commit all sorts of barbarities to swell their coffers, inviting reprisals.

Captain Townley, a colleague of Captain Swan made voyages between Mexico and the Spanish settlements of South America. He joined forces with a band of French buccaneers and carried out a series of raids against the Spanish. There were atrocities committed on both sides during these battles including the beheading of prisoners. Townley died of wounds inflicted on him during one of these raids.

With the proclamation of the king's pardon for all buccaneers who gave up their way of life, it followed that those who did not comply would be hunted down and arrested as pirates, even if the buccaneers activities were directed at the Spanish. The South Sea began to empty of buccaneers and very soon was cleared of them altogether.

The English government, through its colonial governors attempted to restrain the English buccaneers from undertaking any major enterprises. By harsh treatment of a few buccaneers they gave notice that independent actions would be considered piracy. The French government also attempted to reign in their buccaneers, but it was not that easy. If it applied sanctions they might quit Hispaniola, leaving the colony at the mercy of the Spaniards. Only in time of war would the French government find the resources to defend its possessions in the West Indies. The stark truth was that it was cheaper to use the buccaneers. Consequently the French buccaneers continued as before, but limited their activities to the West Indies. The French government still tried to establish more control over their sea-rovers and they did this by absorbing the leaders of the buccaneers into the army and navy. The French hoped that their men would also consent to government discipline. As we have seen, being a leader of buccaneers could be very much a temporary position, the men's independence being well known. The French buccaneers demonstrated this in 1688 when they launched an unprovoked attack on the Danish factory on the island of St Thomas (one of the Virgin Islands to the east of Puerto Rico). They carried away much plunder but failed to locate the main treasure of 500,000 livres which was concealed in a vault. Unusually they did not torture their prisoners to determine the whereabouts of further treasures, probably because they had amassed such plunder that they considered they had taken all the Danes had to offer.

In the same year the English and French authorities had cause to call on the services of the buccaneers again. At the very time they were trying to curb their activities they offered them privateering contracts when war broke out in Europe between France and Spain. England sided with Spain in 1689 which was a shock to both English and French buccaneers. One of the reasons England allied themselves to Spain was of course political, the English coming to an understanding that they had more to fear from the French than the Spanish, hence the English government's attempts to prevent attacks on Spanish settlements by English buccaneers. For nearly two hundred years the English and French buccaneers had co-operated with each other, in a sense doing the dirty work for their respective governments. One would have thought that they would have been reluctant to fight one another, but the fact that they did reveals that really they had no allegiance but to their own self-interest. Being privateers merely meant that they could legally plunder without being labelled as pirates by their respective governments. An added bonus was that they would be treated as prisoners of war if captured, in theory anyway.

Just before England declared war on France, the French attacked St Christopher, the island they had jointly administered since 1625. This reinforced the view of the English government that France was coveting the English colonies in the West Indies and even perhaps the English colonies on the mainland of America. The war was a prolonged one, lasting until 1697 and the buccaneers, now privateers, were employed as auxiliaries to the regular forces on both sides.

It was the end of the buccaneer fraternity.

St Christopher was re-taken by the English. The French also suffered at the hands of the Spaniards in Hispaniola. About five hundred Frenchmen fell in the battle, including De Cussy, the governor of the French part of the island. The town of Cape Fracois was razed to the ground. The French made several raids on Jamaica and although they failed to take it they were able to kidnap a large number of African slaves. The main aim of the war in the West Indies was to seize each other's possessions, but this required total command of the sea by one side or another, and neither could achieve this.

In 1697, at the instigation of M le Baron de Pointis, an officer in the French navy, a large force was sent out from France for an expedition against the Spanish settlements in the West Indies. Commanding the enterprise was M de Pointis himself and orders were sent out to M du Casse, the governor of the French settlements in Hispaniola, to raise twelve hundred men from Tortuga and Hispaniola to supplement the king's men. M du Casse could not raise anything like this number from his regular troops and seamen and he had to call on the French buccaneers to fulfil his quota.

M de Pointis was not the sort of commander the buccaneers were used to. They found him pompous and overbearing and immediately a state of mistrust existed between them. It fell to M du Casse to keep the peace between their commander and themselves, or more accurately to perpetrate a series of confidence tricks upon them. Perhaps it was inevitable that there would be hostility between the authorities and the sea-rovers. The authorities at this time wanted the buccaneers out of their hair, but once again they needed them for the operation ahead. No fools, the buccaneers knew this and tried to extract the best terms possible from M de Pointis and M du Casse, while keeping a weather eye open for possible betrayal.

A large fleet, including eleven frigates was assembled and set sail for Carthagena on the 13th April and the landing took place on the 15th. M de Pointis detailed the buccaneers to take the hill of De la Poupa. Unless the position was secured the defenders would probably have had the time to carry off the treasure of Carthagena to a safe place. No regular forces were involved in this assault, probably because M de Pointis wished to preserve them. It is also likely that a high casualty rate amongst the buccaneers would reduce any future threat to the French authorities. The buccaneers succeeded in their objective which paved the way for the eventual capitulation of the city on the 3rd May.

The terms for the surrender of the city were as follows :-
1.   That all public effects and office accounts should be delivered to the captors.
2.   That merchants should produce their books of accounts, and deliver up All money and effects held by them for their correspondents.
3.   That every inhabitant should be free to leave the city or to remain in his dwelling. That those who retired from the city should first deliver Up all their property there to the captors. That those who chose to Remain should declare faithfully, under penalty of entire confiscation, The gold, silver, and jewels in their possession; on which condition And delivering up one half, they should be permitted to retain the other half and afterwards to be regarded as subjects of France.
4.   That the churches and religious houses should be protected.

The collection of plunder by the authorities did not prevent pillage by the troops and seamen. There were in fact two collections, one official and one unofficial. In other words the treaty was constantly breached. Churches were looted and troops forcibly entered the citizens' homes. When petitioned about these outrages M de Pointis issued instructions that the treaty should be honoured but directed no resources to secure this end. There is little doubt that the buccaneers were heavily involved in these robberies in defiance of the treaty. Inhabitants even hired some of the buccaneers to defend their homes against their comrades and while some honoured their contracts the vast majority looted the house they were paid to defend. Being unable to control them M de Pointis formulated a plan to empty the

The grenade was a weapon much used by buccaneers. Blackbeard used glass grenades during his last sea engagement.

city of the buccaneers. He spread stories that 10,000 Indians were on their way to Carthagena. Always ready for a fight the buccaneers accepted his orders that they should intercept them. They spent several days looking for the non-existent Indians before returning to Carthagena. On arrival the buccaneers found the city fortified against them, the gates guarded by the king's troops. The buccaneers were forced to camp outside the city walls for fifteen days. Meanwhile the treasure was crated and put aboard the king's ships. There was to be no major distribution of the plunder to the buccaneers, settlers or the other people who had helped in the engagement. M du Casse petitioned M de Pointis for justice to be done and eventually he was informed that the share of the plunder due to the colonists, including himself and the buccaneers, would be 400,000 crowns.

The buccaneers had not expected so little reward for putting their lives at risk and playing such a major part in the capture of Carthagena. Not withstanding the fact that some of the buccaneers had already engaged in looting they still felt that they were not getting their fair share of the booty. They were so outraged at their treatment that they seriously planned to board M de Pointis's flagship, the *Sceptre*, a warship of 84 guns. Wiser counsel prevailed and as a body they decided to plunder Carthagena again, but this time without the restraints imposed on them by M de Pointis. On hearing of their intentions M du Casse informed M de Pointis, who was still in harbour, but no action was taken. The ships sailed for France on the 1st June leaving the residents of Carthagena at the mercy of the now uncontrollable buccaneers.

One can but imagine what the residents of Carthagena felt on catching sight of the buccaneers ships returning to the city. Landing unopposed the buccaneers rounded up all the male citizens they could and locked them up in the church. They posted notices around the city informing the inhabitants that the second invasion was a just reaction to their betrayal by their former general. The buccaneers demanded five million livres as the price to be paid to leave Carthagena. It seems beyond reason that the buccaneers expected this sum to be raised so soon after the first plunder, but guessed that much had been hidden by the inhabitants. By putting some to the torture and by other foul means the town raised the amount demanded. The second plunder of Carthagena ended on the buccaneers receiving news from a ship that a powerful fleet of English and Dutch men-of-war had just arrived in the West Indies. Divisions were made of the plunder, including gold, silver, merchandise and slaves.

On arriving in Barbados the commanders of the English and Dutch fleet learned of the French raid on Carthagena. The fleet sailed immediately to attack them, and came in sight of the French fleet leaving Carthagena for France. They gave chase but failed to engage them. At the beginning of June the French buccaneers sailed from Carthagena in nine ships making for Hispaniola. They crossed the path of the Allied fleet and two of their ships most heavily laden with treasure were taken. Two more were driven ashore and wrecked, one of them close to Carthagena. The crew were captured by the Spanish and expected rough treatment on account of their atrocities committed on the inhabitants of Carthagena. However, they were treated as prisoners of war and made to work on the rebuilding of the fortifications. The five other ships made good their escape. This was the last major enterprise of the buccaneers in the Caribbean. The long war between England and France was ended in September by the *Treaty of Ryswick*. One of the conditions was that the former French part of the island of St Christopher was restored to them.

English and French buccaneers were under severe pressure from now on to disband and to submit themselves to good governance. Some became planters or settled amongst the native population. Others returned to their respective countries or colonies, but a hard core became pirates, preying on ships of any nation.

Rivalry between England and France soon led to another conflict just four years after the *Treaty of Ryswick.* This became known as the *War of the Spanish Succession (1701-1713).* One of the first acts by the English was to drive out the French from St Christopher, this time for good. Privateers were still used during this war but under stricter control and not all of them were former buccaneers. Many privateer ships were crewed from Bristol. Edward Drummond of Bristol came to prominence as a privateer during the *War of the Spanish Succession,* changing his name to Tache or Teach during the conflict. Whether Teach acquired a taste for plunder or whether he felt cast aside by the authorities after the war, he turned pirate at war's end. Known as Blackbeard, he is probably the pirate that first springs to mind when the subject is discussed, together with the fictional character of Long John Silver. Blackbeard's life, or as much that is known about it, will be discussed in Part 2 of this narrative. James Burney, who made a study of the buccaneers activities states that ….

In the history of so much robbery and outrage the rapacity shown in some instances by the European governments in their West India transaction, and by governors of their appointment, appears in a worse light than that of the buccaneers, from whom, they being professed ruffians, nothing better was expected. The superior attainments of Europeans, though they have done much towards their own civilisation, chiefly in humanising their institutions have, in their dealings with the inhabitants of the rest of the globe, with few exceptions, been made the instruments of usurpation and extortion.

After the suppression of the buccaneers, and partly from their relics, arose a race of pirates of a more desperate cast, so rendered by the increased danger of their occupation, who for a number of years preyed upon the commerce of all nations, till they were hunted down and, it may be said, exterminated. Of one crew of pirates who were brought before a court of justice, fifty-two men were condemned and executed at one time in the year 1722.

Ken Griffiths.

A 17th century warship.

Part 2: Of Admirals, Adventurers and the Pirate Pinnacle.

Bristol Beginnings

On the edge of ancient civilisation, Britain was considered a land of mists and fog. Capable of being a thorn in the side of Roman world domination, this strange, wealthy isle assisted the Gauls in their fights for freedom. Early traders had explored the seaways around the country from antiquity. The Severn Sea, gateway to old Bristol was treated with trepidation; swirling seas, wicked winds and a treacherous tidal range compounded the danger for anyone brave enough to risk the journey.

Navigable up a sweeping gorge, the settlement that was to become the metropolis of the West was at first difficult to tame. 8 nautical miles from the sea a mass of water would forcibly ebb and flow through a deep ravine cut by the last ice age, meeting the downward thrust of two rivers, the Avon and the Frome that flowed through a verdant valley that was surrounded by seven hills. In between these high spots, marshes had formed and woodland flourished with oak, alder and hazel trees.
Iron Age hill forts on each side of the gorge protected the

Gorge of Avon with pit-dwellings on Downs.

entrance to this haven, but the might of the Roman Empire, when it was finally unleashed, overwhelmed the peoples of the Dubini and Cangi despite these tribes putting up a spirited resistance. The legions were then able to use the area as a staging post to quash the Welsh resistance across the Severn.

On realising the potential of their conquered land in the West the Romans developed their staging post into an important port later known as Sea Mills, using it to export goods such as lead from the Mendips and grain from the Cotswolds. To access the port they built a major road north and parallel of the Avon, crossing the Frome at what is now Wade Street Bridge, effectively bypassing the troublesome confluence of Bristol's two major rivers. The road ran to Aquae Sulis (Bath), at that time becoming an important capital within the Empire.

The departure of Rome's legions led to the gradual encroachment of the West Saxons into the region. The settlement of Brygstowe, Saxon for *the place by the bridge,* was established with a street layout forming a cross on top of a mound standing over the confluence to the Avon and the Frome. One of these arteries came away towards a crossing point bridging the Avon at its meeting with the Frome, connecting the growing hamlet with Redcliffe.

Legend has it that Alfred the Great, during his escape from the Danes, sought refuge in Redcliffe's caves. He went on to unify the kingdom and create England's first navy. The remnants of the defeated Danes turned to piracy on the coast of Wessex and Alfred smashed them with his superior galleys, some propelled by over sixty rowers. After Alfred's death in 889 the Anglo-Saxons continued to have strife with the Danes and Vikings based in Dublin, and throughout this period Bristol's defences grew, some historians even claiming that an early castle had been built. Certainly by the end of the 10th Century a mint had been established and silver coins minted in Bristol made it to Denmark as part of the infamous 'Danegeld'.

The coming of the Normans brought dramatic changes to Bristol. Whilst the Romans never fully exploited Bristol's location, and the Saxons kept it as an unruly border town, the Normans realised its full potential immediately and set about reinforcing its defences and utilising its strategic location. The town's old wooden castle was remodelled and they started protecting the town's shipping with outer defences. Bristol grew quickly during this period, but hardly noticed, the Domesday Book of 1086 failing to note much of what was going on.

Bishop Wulfstan of Worcester, who was responsible for the compilation of the Book locally, was well aware of the traffic in slaves however (a trade that had been going on for over 400 hundred years between Bristol and Ireland) and he preached regularly for its suppression. The slave traders were ruthless; in addition to taking the offspring of the poor, they would kidnap people and even put the women in the family way if it added to their profits. One of the miracles attributed to Saint Wulfstan, as he later became, was the ending of this nefarious trade. He would preach every Sunday for months on end against the trade; he petitioned King William and achieved the support of Lanfranc, Bishop of Canterbury, to aid his cause. Ultimately he was successful and in the first recorded instance of a mob rising in Bristol, they took the eyes of one of the slave traders to celebrate, an act not condoned by St Wulfstan, but it does demonstrate the hostility felt by the people who had suffered at the hands of the slave traders. Another of Wulfstan's stated miracles was the saving of a storm tossed Bristol ship bound for Dublin.

Under the Normans Bristol prospered; they carried on fortifying the town and it had much Royal patronage. The future King Henry II spent his formative years here and when king he gave Dublin to his Bristol backers. This was something of a poisoned chalice though, as the Dubliners rebelled one Easter Monday murdering the English colonists. The early 13th Century saw Bristol really expand, with the replacement in stone of the old wooden Bristol Bridge. The early Saxon settlement was physically united with the prospering Redcliffe and Temple parishes much to their chagrin. Bristol Castle was given the second mightiest keep in the Kingdom, and construction started on one of the greatest feats of medieval engineering, the cutting of the massive 'Frome Trench'. This half mile stretch of the re-routed river Frome doubled Bristol's capacity for shipping and made her one of the greatest ports in the country – for the next 500 years.

Trade massively increased in the 13th and 14th centuries with Bristol ships exporting wool and woollen goods and importing wine. Some merchants were corrupt and were dishonest in their dealings, so much so that a saying developed …. *That if you shake hands with A Bristolian – count your fingers afterwards.* All the while, Bristol played a key role in national events. Edward I used the town as a launch pad for his domination of the Welsh; Edward II was taken from Bristol to his grisly demise at Berkeley Castle and Edward III relied on Bristol ships and Bristol men to help him with his siege of Calais. He was so grateful he granted Bristol Town and County status in 1373.

One of the reasons Bristol's port was so popular was because it was a safe haven from pirates, early references showing that Lundy was a popular base for these sea rovers. From this stronghold they mounted attacks on anything and everything from Cornwall in the South to Gloucestershire in the North, the Welsh coast and as far away as Ireland. One of the robber lords of Lundy, William de Marisco, was implicated in an attempted assassination of Henry III by a clerk named Richard who pretended to be a jester in his court. He was discovered under the king's bed with a long knife and he was immediately dragged off (literally at the tails of horses) from Woodstock to Oxford to be hanged.

Marisco escaped to Lundy and carried on with his *piracy and rapine* until he was captured along with 16 accomplices during a surprise attack. They were immediately taken to the Tower where they were hung, drawn and quartered, the first recorded English incident of this nature. Their severed bodies were sent to the four principle cities of the kingdom *to strike terror into all beholders*. Despite the perils of piracy, Bristol merchants thrived during this period and one of them, William Canynge built up the largest fleet of privately owned vessels in the kingdom, if not Europe.

The end of the fifteenth century saw Bristol as a centre for world exploration. Henry VII gave a Royal Warrant to Genoan born Venetian Giovanni Cabotto (anglicised to John Cabot) to discover a new route to the Indies, whereupon in his little Bristol ship the *Matthew* he located the mainland of North America in 1497. It wasn't by chance that Cabot came to Bristol to make his voyage. Bristol's hardy Icelandic cod fishers were renowned throughout Europe and Christopher Columbus was among those who consulted with them before making his epic voyage.

The early 16th Century saw continued piracy, especially in the Mediterranean. A Plymouth captain, John Rawlings was captured by Algerian pirates and sold as a slave, then put to work on a captured Bristol ship named the *Exchange.* He mutinied with some fellow slaves, threw his captors overboard and brought the ship safely home to Bristol.

Cabot's son, Bristol born Sebastian, claimed he had accompanied his father on his voyage in the *Matthew,* but was luckily absent when the follow up trip was made. It

The trade mark of William Canynge.

is said that when exploring America's eastern seaboard Cabot senior and crew fell in with some hostile Spaniards and 'disappeared'. No one will ever know exactly what happened to them. Sebastian had many other adventures, apparently a more talented cartographer than a leader of men; he entered the Spanish service, first exploring the River Plate for them (when he should have been following Magellan's route) and then leading an expedition to Brazil in 1526, both with mixed results.

For the next eleven years Sebastian became an examiner of Spanish pilots. In 1544 he drew a world map for Ortelius, the renowned map maker from Antwerp. Four years later he was invited back to England and granted a royal pension with the title 'Grand Pilot of England', becoming a life governor for the Company of Merchant Venturers formed in 1551. When trade stagnated due to a war on the continent he sent Chancellor and Willoughby to open up new trade with Russia, who, under Ivan the Terrible, were happy to deal with the English as they saw it as a good way to break up the Hanseatic League's monopoly. Sebastian Cabot was the first Englishman to promote ships sheathing for protection, his favoured material being lead! He died in 1565.

By the middle of the 16th Century Bristol was rich enough to provide twelve ships to assist Henry VIII's siege of Boulogne. Bristol had its own bishopric and mint and was proclaimed a city. It was also developing its privateering interests.

With the coming of Elizabeth I, Bristol became a more important place, on the 'Queen's Progress' of 1574 the city even had a convention named after it. The 'Convention of Bristol' was a timely piece of diplomacy between England and Spain which called for both countries to stop harbouring aliens unfriendly to one another, to afford the Netherlands greater liberties and to prevent

Sebastien Cabot

intention to invest 1000 marks and two ships of 60 and 40 tons, *for discoveries on the coast of America.* The leader of the expedition was Sir Humphrey Gilbert who tried to colonise Newfoundland, a contributor to the start of the British Empire. He perished in the icy waters of the North Atlantic on his return home in the overloaded ship *Squirrel,* which went down with all hands, this was apparently due to undue greed – prompted by overloading and encouraged by the promoter.

By the time of the Spanish Armada in 1588, Bristol was ready to answer the call of the realm once more and sent four ships, the *Great Unicorne,* the *Minion,* the *Handmaide,* and the *Ayde,* well furnished with men and ammunition to join the rest of the fleet at Plymouth. All of the canvas brought to St James's Fair was bought to make tents for the Queen's army camped at Tilbury, this shows the importance of the Fair which was one of the biggest in Western Europe.

During the same year as James I's arrival to the English throne in 1603 Alderman Aldworth and Alderman Whitson financed an expedition to explore America. Under command of 23 year old Martin Prinn or Pring, the 50 ton *Speedwell* and the 26 ton *Discoverer* sailed from Bristol with orders to find the North West Passage. They took with them the following goods for barter....*light goods, caps of divers colours, kerseys, tools, beads and bugles (long, slender glass beads, usually black).* The voyage went fair and they rounded Cape Cod and on into Massachusetts Bay, anchoring at 'Whitson Bay', later to be renamed 'Plymouth Harbour' by the Pilgrim Fathers. A nearby mount was christened 'Mount Aldworth' and the expedition stayed there for a few weeks, at one time warding off an attack from the natives with their two great mastiffs, 'Fool' and 'Gallant'. They managed to find a valuable medicinal herb called Sassafras, the root of which they shipped home along with much vital information.

the Inquisition from further molesting English sailors. Elizabeth had to promise to discourage her seamen from raiding King Philip of Spain's commerce as pirates or privateers. This was a bit awkward for Francis Drake who had just come home from another successful cruise of the Spanish Main and he had to lie low.

In 1582, wealthy merchant and mayor, Thomas Aldworth advised the Queen's right hand man, Walsingham of his

Alderman John Whitson.

Pring went on to become one of England's foremost seafarers, not only for this exploration but also for his East India voyages. He died in 1626 and is buried in St. Stephen's church, surmounted by the arms of the Merchant Venturers with numerous allegorical figures in allusion to his profession, along with an inscription to his life.

James I issued a patent to the 'Plymouth Company', consisting of interested parties from Bristol, Plymouth and Exeter for the colonisation of that part of America called Ancient Norumbega, or Northern Virginia, lying between 38 and 45 degrees north. Pring was sent on another voyage, this time financed by Sir Fernando Gorges and Sir John Popham, but little is known about it, other than maintaining the financier's interest in colonisation. In 1620 the Pilgrim Fathers entered negotiations with the company in order to gain transport across the Atlantic.

In 1609, John Guy set forth with some colonists to set up a plantation in Newfoundland but the venture ended in failure because of its inability to exert any authority over pirates that used the island for refitting or over fishermen of other nations. Another colony set up nearby by John Barker in 1618 proved more successful however, and the colony of 'Bristol Hope at Harbour Grace' came into being.

Running parallel to Bristol's efforts at colonisation, Jamestown was established in the early 1600s by a London expedition and was Britain's first colony on the American mainland. It survived primarily due to the efforts of Thomas de la Warr and the introduction of tobacco. Descended from an old Wickwar family, renowned for their soldierly skills, de la Warr prevented Jamestown's abandonment and subsequently had the Delaware tribe, river and state all named after him. The fledgling colony was founded in 1607, when famous people such as Captain John Smith and Pocahontas helped with its formation. The first shipments of African slaves arrived in 1619 and by 1698 the London monopoly was broken leading to Bristol's legal involvement.

When Captain John Powell landed on Barbados in 1624, with his London backed expedition, he immediately claimed it for England and thereafter it became a thriving colony, initially growing tobacco and then sugar. Other Caribbean Islands followed, St Kitts, also in 1624 and amazingly shared with the French, Nevis in 1628 and Antigua, Barbuda and Montserrat all in 1632. Bristol merchants were immediately attracted there and set up plantations in large numbers. With sugar came the need for a large workforce and initially these jobs were filled by indentured servants, impoverished white people who had the same status as slaves; these were known as 'Red Legs' and were of English, Irish and Scottish descent. The

Spanish had already worked the native peoples to death and were replacing them with African slaves, a process quickly adopted by the other European powers. It was said that the annual wealth created by Nevis alone amounted to more than the combined gross domestic product of all of Britain's 13 American colonies. Little wonder it was a target for pirates as well as other nations.

The Spanish didn't take the loss of their possessions lying down and many islands changed hands on a regular basis and interlopers were dealt with harshly. It is recorded in 1628 that a Captain Samuel Pitts on a passage from Jamaica to Bristol bravely defended his ship *Kirtlington Gally* against a mighty Spanish Rover. The Society of Merchant Venturers gave him a *richly chased silver monteith and collar* as a reward for his actions. This engagement took place during England's war with Spain that ran between1625 and 1630; it also gave us the *Angel Gabriel* ballad featured at the start of this book.

One of the most eventful voyages was that of Captain Thomas James, a former barrister, who proved to be a resourceful and intrepid seaman. Backed by members of Bristol's Corporation, he set out in May 1631 to *discover a passage by the North-West into the Southern Seas, to visit Japan, and to round the world Westward, and so once more arrive at home.* His ship was the 70 ton *Henrietta Maria,* named after Charles I's wife; he had a crew of twenty men and two boys with enough provisions for 18 months and they reached Greenland within a month before terrible weather and ice packs nearly wrecked them. They actually struck an iceberg but found salvation on nearby rocks where they managed to fashion some repairs.

Undeterred they pressed on, meeting a London expedition led by Captain Foxe in August, who had set out with the same purpose as the Bristol men; Foxe ridiculed James' intention of carrying on but while he returned

A portrait of Captain James.

home to anonymity, James went on to 'undying fame'. They entered the Hudson Bay and spent three months desperately seeking the North-West passage, working farther and farther South, until reaching the Bay that still bears his name…. *They were the first, that ever burst, Into that silent sea.*

Sensing the impending winter, and knowing that their entrance into the Hudson Bay was now already frozen over, James' men built themselves a shelter ashore, complete with a kitchen and a roof made of sailcloth. By October they had the presence of mind to sink the *Henriette Maria* in shallow water near the shore to prevent her from being crushed by the expected ice. Prior to scuttling her they had lost an anchor and the ship's rudder in bad weather and had to probe around in the ice with lances before reuniting them with the ship. They had a miserable time and despite having plenty of firewood they were still frozen inside their shelter; their diet was salt junk, salt fish and biscuit. For drink they melted snow. Scurvy broke out and three of the crew died before they discovered some green vetches in June of the following year.

Just after their ship was re-floated, James was taking observations up a tall tree when one of his crew accidentally set fire to some low lying bushes. An inferno soon started and they only just escaped with their lives, racing back to their camp to warn the others. Before the flames engulfed them they managed to strip the sails off the roof of their shelter and transfer the powder and stores back to the *Henrietta Maria*.

James wanted to carry on searching for the North-West passage for another season but his men had had enough, not wanting to end up like Henry Hudson twenty years before, cast away in an open boat. They set sail for home, arriving back in Bristol in October 1632. Prior to departure, James had declared the new territory for Charles I and this bore fruit in 1670 when the Hudson Bay Company was formed to develop the fur trade in the James Bay area. Not quite such good news for the beavers, however. The last that was heard of Thomas James was that he did good service against the Turkish pirates and the Spaniards.

In 1632, two of James' backers, Robert Aldworth and Giles Elbridge, were given a patent of 12,000 acres of land in New England and an additional 100 acres for every extra person that they transported there until 1639. There was a three year qualifying period and it's not known how many people took up the offer, but it certainly demonstrates that they were keen to colonise.

The next decade saw the advent of the Civil War and although Bristol tried to remain neutral during the conflict, the city with its port and strategic position dictated against this. Bristol was battered by both sides and the people suffered much hardship. It was just after Cromwell's re-occupation of the city that the castle was razed to the ground. As the war progressed, Bristol's merchants began to trade again when in 1648 the King's Scottish army was defeated; several merchants came forward to transport 500 prisoners into slavery on the plantations in the West Indies and Virginia. More Scots prisoners followed three years later after another Royalist defeat; and during Cromwell's re-conquest of Ireland hundreds of Irish prisoners ended up in such places as Barbados, all through the port of Bristol.

Events outside Bristol continued to influence the city's fate; Charles I was executed and Cromwell established his Commonwealth, notably acquiring Jamaica in 1655. On Cromwell's death five years later, his son lacked the necessary wit and guile required to succeed and Parliament consequently asked Charles II to take the throne. The cycle of war and peace continued with nations swapping affinity at the drop of a hat and people like Henry Morgan using it as an excuse for their own personal gain.

It was with James II's accession to the throne in February 1685 that the spotlight of the country would focus on events in the West, ending in Judge Jeffreys *The Western Martyrdom, or Bloody Assizes*. The new king was a Roman Catholic and unpopular from the start; up step James, Duke of Monmouth and Buccleuch, illegitimate son of Charles II, handsome, athletic and successful with women, he was also brainless, vain, ungovernable and ambitious. He landed at Lyme on June 1st and was proclaimed King at Taunton on June 10th – the Pitchfork Rebellion was about to begin, with the Pretender swelling his army with untrained labourers.

Monmouth's first target was England's second city, Bristol, but it never quite happened. He got his rag tag army to Keynsham and actually crossed the County Bridge into Gloucestershire but didn't press home his advantage. This cost him dear and he took a circuitious route back to Sedgemoor and was soundly beaten on July 6th by James' professional army led by the Earl of Faversham and Lord Churchill (the latter, a former Recorder of Bristol who went on to become one of the foremost Generals on the world stage as the Duke of Marlborough).

It was a massacre, the King lost about 30 men killed and just over 200 wounded while at least 1,400 of Monmouth's men died in the fighting and pursuit. The rebels were tracked down by Colonel Kirke and his battle hardened men (they had just retuned from a campaign in Tunisia). Known as 'Kirke's Lambs' they were noted for their savagery, who hung or slaughtered anyone they caught. This wasn't enough for James who wanted a 'fuller vengeance', recalling Kirke and appointing Chief Justice Jefferys. This man would broker no defence and abused those he sentenced…. *Altogether 233 persons were hanged, quartered, and gibbeted in various parts of the county [Somerset], cross-roads, market places and village greens being rendered pestiferous by decomposing corpses….*

About 850 rebels, the lucky ones, if you can call them that, were transported to the West Indies to join the Red Legs and work as slaves; most were shipped out through Bristol.

Jeffreys arrived in Bristol in September and started his assize with the following statement…. *Rebellion was like the sin of witchcraft, and Bristol had too many rebels who had added to the ship's lading.* To his great annoyance only six could be found, of whom three were reprieved and three hung on Redcliffe Hill. He then switched his assault to the city's Magistrates. For thirty years they had commuted death sentences to transportation for life to work on Plantations in the Americas and in so doing made profits from this slave labour which they pooled and shared out.

Jefferys accused the Mayor of Bristol and 5 others of being *kidnapping knaves* and even ordered the mayor to get into the witness box, where he vented his spleen, afterwards quietly pocketing the compensation money paid for their offences. Jefferys' modus operandi was to hang the poor and sell pardons to the rich. His reign of terror only lasted three more years; when he tried to follow his master James II into exile during the 'Glorious Revolution' he was captured and placed in the Tower of London where he died before he could be brought to trial. The Wapping collier on which he tried to escape (disguised as a sailor) contained over 35,000 guineas and much silver plate.

As a footnote, General Wade, who served with Monmouth, turned informer and sought King James II's favour by betraying his former comrades who took part in the rebellion; he was granted property which he developed around what is now Wade Street, building a new bridge on the site of a Roman one that to this day is known as 'Traitor's Bridge'.

Admirals of the West

The most famous admiral ever to come out of Bristol was Admiral Sir William Penn, who, along with naval secretary and diarist Samuel Pepys, is credited with being the founder of our modern navy. He was the son of Bristol sea captain and merchant Giles Penn and his beautifully restored arms testify to his small size while the victory pennants taken from the Dutch testify to his great courage. These can be seen today, high up in St Mary Redcliffe church, not far from where he is buried.

He is more widely known today as the father of Quaker William Penn who has been given the credit of being the founder of the American State of Pennsylvania. In fact the state is named after Admiral Penn. The land was granted to the Penn family in lieu of the debt King Charles II owed him. The Penn's were a fairly wealthy family originally from Wiltshire and Giles was the first to go to sea where he rose in rank, dying in the Mediterranean whilst ambassador to one of the states there. Giles Penn's greatest achievement however was his contribution against the Barbary Pirates.

From the 16th Century onwards these Turkish corsairs (as they were known at the time) were a persistent thorn in the side to all of the European powers; their favourite trick being to snatch people away and hold them for ransom, but if this proved 'un-commercial', they used them as galley slaves or worse. By the early 17th Century large fleets of them were based in the Bristol Channel, attacking all and sundry, threatening England's Newfoundland fleet and even visitors to Bristol's annual St James's fair. Reports about their activities came from as far away as Penzance, their Mayor famously asking for assistance at one time.

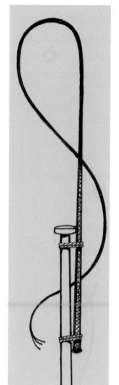

In 1635, after 5 Turkish ships wreaked havoc in the 'Severne', Giles petitioned King Charles I to raid the Moroccan base of Sallee. The following year the king dispatched Captain Rainsborough with a fleet of 4 ships and they destroyed 28 ships hemmed into the port. The Governor sued for peace and hundreds of English and Irish slaves were freed and returned home. Some had been missing for 30 years. In celebration the former slaves were paraded at night through London dressed in white robes – there were so many it was said to be *like daylight*. A treaty was signed to the effect that the pirates had to desist from their activities, but within a few years the whole of Britain was in turmoil with the advent of the English Civil War and the corsairs quietly went back to their old business, a trait that came easy due to the constant power struggles within Europe.

The Penn family, like virtually every other at this time had their loyalties tested; Giles's son William became a parliamentarian and fought alongside the brilliant Bridgwater Admiral Robert Blake; and Rainsborough also turned against his old master, leading part of the army that retook Bristol for the Protectorate. It was with Blake that the future Admiral Penn's military career took off. First against the Royalists and again when the Commonwealth found itself at war with the Dutch.

In one of his famous encounters with Admiral Van Tromp, the Dutchman tied a broom to his masthead and implied that he had *swept the Channel of the English fleet*. In response, Vice-Admiral Penn sent a riding-whip up to his masthead *to let the braggart know that they were going to flog him back to Holland;* after three day's fight they did so.

In 1655, as part of Cromwell's 'Western Design', an expedition was sent to the West Indies to take Hispaniola for the Commonwealth; Penn was Admiral of the fleet, whilst General Robert Venables was in charge of 2,500 soldiers. The commanders argued and the operation descended into farce. The force, although large, was badly led, manned by rejects from other regiments, augmented by undisciplined and cowardly planters. Venables was twice surprised by ambush in the same place and before a major attack on San Domingo could take place the force went down with dysentery after eating oranges that were a substitute for the lack of water bottles.

They left without even attacking their target and occupied Jamaica by way of compensation. Even this didn't go well though as the Spaniards, who took to the hills, took some time to subdue. These were to become the latter day Maroons. The consolation prize didn't please Cromwell either who promptly had both leaders slung into the Tower. When Admiral Penn was having his adventure in the West Indies, his mentor, Robert Blake, was blazing his way to glory with several victories against the Spanish and the pirates of Tunis. He died of injuries at sea in 1657 and was buried with full honours in Westminster Abbey. Unfortunately, at the Restoration, Charles II had Blake's body exhumed and dumped into a commoner's grave.

Ironically it was Penn who helped restore the king to the throne, fetching him from the continent in the *Naesby*, later renamed the *Royal Charles* in 1660. Furthermore, it was in this vessel that Penn served as Captain of the Fleet five years later at the battle of Lowestoft under Charles II's brother James (the future King). This was to be Penn's last great naval engagement when the Dutch were soundly beaten. During the last decade of his life Penn moved to London actually living next door to Samuel Pepys and it was here that they moulded together modern naval strategies. These had been originally laid down by Robert Blake. There are many amusing moments between

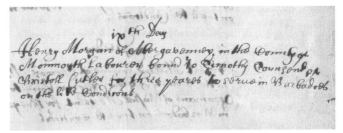

Morgan's signature on his indenture document c/o BRO.

the two men during this period and they've come down to us in Pepys' diary, including their escape together from the Great Fire of London in 1666. Admiral Penn continued to act as a Commissioner for the Navy until his death four years after the Great Fire at the age of 49.

According to Henry Morgan's entry in the Indentured Servants Book at Bristol Records Office, he was born in Abergavenney, Wales, to a military family with two uncles who were successful soldiers of fortune. They fought on opposite sides during the English Civil War, Thomas for the parliamentarians, rising to the rank of major-general in the New Model Army, and Edward for the Royalists. After a period of exile before the Restoration, Edward became deputy governor of Jamaica.

Henry left school early and is quoted as saying being *more used to pike than book.* None would have predicted his rise to Admiral and Colonial Governor. In early 1655 he ended up being shipped from Bristol to become an apprentice cutler to Timothy Townsend (a Bristol man himself) in Barbados. Life as a servant on a foreign plantation apparently didn't agree with him and he promptly escaped to serve as a subaltern in Cromwell's 'Western Design', sailing under Admiral Penn.

He did well and after Jamaica was taken. Morgan became a captain in the Jamaican Port Royal Regiment and given a ship with a privateering commission, sailing with Christopher Myngs on his raid on Puerto Del Principe.

Here he first showed his genius as a military strategist, but booty was scarce, and his fellow troops were dissatisfied. Over the next few years he followed up his earlier successes with a brutal raid on Porto Bello, Panama, where he and his buccaneers massacred and tortured the garrison.

After many scrapes he held a meeting of the pirate kings on his flagship, *HMS Oxford,* but disaster struck when a spark from some revellers lit the powder magazine and the vessel blew up killing many, but sparing Morgan. The Spanish thought it was just retribution and the work of their Virgin Mary sculpture in Cartagena. Apparently the sculpture's eyes flowed with tears after the event – a miracle that made her even more venerated. Although not a brilliant seaman, Morgan's reputation as a commander was not in question. In 1669 he led a famous victory at the Bar of Maracaibo where he attacked the Spanish flagship Magdalena; she exploded after Morgan had set her ablaze with a fire ship.

The highlight of his career was leading a band of 2,000 English and French pirates against the rich port of Spanish held Panama in 1670/1671. He achieved this remarkable feat by crossing the Isthmus with a forced starvation march. After sacking the city and with allegations that he had tortured his hostages, Morgan returned to the Caribbean and made off with most of the loot. Unknown to him though he lost the richest prize – the Cathedral's solid gold altarpiece had been whitewashed by a cunning Friar.

On his return from Panama the political climate changed and Morgan was made to return to London to answer charges of piracy (of all things!). At home though he was treated as a hero and despite being under arrest, he led life in his usual manner, repeatedly exonerated due to his popularity. King Charles II even knighted him, although he complained privately that Jamaica had become *a Christian Algiers.* After another political u-turn, Morgan was sent back to Jamaica to take up the appointment of Lieutenant Governor. Then under the King's orders, he proceeded to hang every pirate he could find, including his former henchmen, a classic case of poacher turned gamekeeper. Later on, Henry was dismissed from official duties due to his heavy drinking in Port Royal's taverns. At the time he was described by Sir Hans Sloane (later founder of the British Museum) as *lean, sallow coloured, his eyes a little yellowish and belly jutting out – much given to drinking and sitting up late.*

Despite being treated by a voodoo man or *obeah* (he had a poultice of clysters of urine plastered all over him with clay and water which did augment his cough), Henry Morgan died in 1688 leaving his wife of 20 years with a huge sugar plantation, £5000 and a multitude of rumours regarding treasure hordes. His body was carried through the streets on a gun carriage and was buried in the church he helped to found, St Peter's. In the 1920s Morgan was described by author George Wycherly as *a depraved, vicious, treacherous, almost unparalleled human brute, who was born of respectable people in Wales but deliberately chose the most evil life possible in this vicious age.*

Little seems to be known about the other great 17th and early 18th Century Admiral to come out of Bristol; his name was William Whetstone. Early details are very sketchy and no one seems to know where he was born or when. It's rumoured that his father served with Penn in Jamaica and others say that like his son-in-law, Woodes Rogers, he had family in Poole. What is known though is that he was earmarked for great things along with his friend and contemporary John Benbow. To a lesser extent, Whetstone's life mirrored that of Benbow's, both tried their hand at privateering and both rose high in the Navy, Benbow always the senior, in terms of age, rank and derring-do.

Benbow's early life is well known. Son of a tanner from Shrewsbury, he was born in 1653 and ran away from home at an early age to become a waterman on the River Severn. He went to sea and soon advanced, becoming master's mate in 1678 and master of the *Nonsuch* the following year. Although brave, he had a reputation for recklessness and was court-martialled for insulting a fellow officer. He immediately became a privateer, first based in London and then Bristol. When in command of the *Malaga Merchant* he was attacked by a Sallee pirate and, turning defence into attack, he promptly beat off the rover. It's said that he cut off and salted the heads of 13 Moors left on his ship and took them to Cadiz where he received a handsome reward from the grateful Spanish. Benbow rejoined the navy as Controller of H.M. Dockyard at Chatham, but this didn't stop him joining in with engagements against the French, one of which being to mortar bomb the privateers of St Malo. This was very successful, but when he tried the same trick against Dunkirk the method failed.

After the *Peace of Ryswick* in 1697 he was sent to the West Indies to address the perennial problem of pirates, in particular the pursuit of New York based Scotsman William Kidd, but the pirate managed to evade him. Benbow then became embroiled in politics during the Darien Project fiasco*, but he managed to escape without any blame. King William III then called for Honest Benbow to protect his interests in the West Indies against the French. Admiral Benbow was on station for about a year before the famous French Admiral Du Casse approached, but when the attack came he found his colleagues lacking. The great man suffered many personal injuries, including losing one of his legs in an encounter that the British should have won. To his aid came acting Rear Admiral (later Sir) William Whetstone, who took over active command of the theatre when Benbow was incapacitated.

* *Scotland's attempt at colonisation.*

Before this, and while Benbow was having his contretemps with various corsairs, Whetstone served a seven year apprenticeship before commanding his first vessel, a merchantman sailing between Bristol, Barbados and Virginia. He then spent 3 years in the Navy but, despite being a 'Good Man', he was laid off before taking command of the Bristol privateer *Delavall* against the French. This turned out to be a brief sojourn as he was soon recalled to the Navy where he advanced quickly, becoming commander of *HMS Dreadnought* on the Newfoundland fishing station for 3 years . He then returned home and was asked to go to Benbow's aid in Jamaica; this was not an easy task as storms and the poor conditions of his squadron's ships made it a long journey. They met up at Port Royal and Whetstone was immediately sent to cruise off Hispaniola in search of Du Casse with the local rank of rear-admiral.

As we have seen, Benbow found his man first and was so furious with his own commander's conduct he demanded a court martial. He was too ill to conduct the trial himself so Whetstone took over and four captains were charged; of these, Hudson died before reaching Jamaica, Constable was thrown out of the Navy and imprisoned at Her Majesty's pleasure (and dying there), while Captains Kirkby and Wade were condemned to death.

Benbow died of his wounds and for six months Whetstone assumed command of his flagship *HMS Bristol* until Benbow's replacement arrived. *HMS Bristol* was then despatched to Britain with Kirkby and Wade aboard; their execution took place off Spithead where they were shot – the Royal Navy refused to allow them to contaminate English soil. The reason their conduct was deemed so bad was because Jean Baptiste Du Casse and his comrades were the ultimate prize; in 1697 they had emulated Morgan's achievement by taking Cartagena with its numerous riches.

It's thought that in an age where naval commissions were bought, Benbow's rise from common stock went against him. Lord Tennyson wrote….

Then they look'd at him they hated
Had what they desired:
Mute with folded arms they waited –
Not a gun was fired

Those, in whom he had reliance
For his noble name,
With one smile of still defiance
Sold him into shame.

Robert Louis Stevenson remembered Admiral Benbow as well by using his name for the inn of that name in the opening sequences of *Treasure Island.*

Before Whetstone returned to Britain he engaged and destroyed several enemy privateers off of San Domingo. His good conduct had reached the ears of 'the powers that be' and when he came home he was officially promoted to Rear Admiral by Prince George - although this caused a bit of a hoo-hah because other Captains claimed seniority. His reward was a squadron in the English Channel and one of his actions here brought him to the attention of Daniel Defoe. Whetstone was promoted again to Commander-in-Chief of the West Indies and undertook lots of diplomatic work to try and get Cuba and Cartegena to declare for King Charles of Spain. Attempts to war with the French were hampered by the sick health of his crews and the poor state of his ships.

Whetstone returned home again in 1706 and took what was to become his final command in 1707, patrolling off Dunkirk to try and control the notorious French corsair Claude de Forbin. He was tasked with escort duty of 19 ships of the Moscovy Company, with orders to guard them as far as the Shetland Islands. This he did, to the letter, but then disaster struck. Forbin, unobserved by Whetstone, overtook the convoy and captured as prizes all but 4 of the fleet. A trial was immediately convened but even though the Admiralty defended his actions he was eventually made the scapegoat. He was dismissed from command and given no further employment.

He died in 1711, owed over £2,500 from various debtors and he was buried in his home town of Bristol in St Michael's Church. At the end of his life French privateers had killed one of his sons and captured a ship he'd owned. His grandson was to die off the same African coast as Alexander Selkirk and the real Israel Hands.

A favourite staple food of the Buccaneers, this much abused creature went on to become a major delicacy on the bill of fare for many famous Bristol Inns including the Bush Tavern in Corn Street.

18th Century woodcut depicting Robinson Crusoe from a Chapbook of the period. Chapbooks were a way of disseminating popular literature in an abridged form and circulated by pedlars or 'chapmen'.

The Adventurers

Bristol's early Adventurers had their exploits celebrated in ballad, song and verse, but with the coming of the 18th Century, a new phenomena was about to sweep the world – the adventure novel, and Bristol exploits were in the vanguard. In 1708, during the War of the Spanish Succession, a group of Bristol Adventurers led by Dampier, Dover and Rogers set out to seize a Manila treasure ship and in so doing discovered and rescued Alexander Selkirk, the original goatskin clad maroon. This discovery inspired Daniel Defoe to write *Robinson Crusoe* in 1719 and with that, spawned a whole succession of literary work that has kept readers enthralled to this day.

The voyage hit the jackpot in other ways as well, not only bringing home the treasure and its ship, most of the original crew and the two vessels they started out with, but also Spanish maps and charts that fuelled the South Sea Bubble, leading to the mother of all stock market scandals and ruining many people. To further put the expedition into perspective, only two other Englishmen ever achieved this feat, Thomas Cavendish in Elizabethan times and Lord Anson in the 1740s. Anson's voyage was backed by the Royal Navy although he lost most of his men and only one of his original six ships returned home, but he became very wealthy.

Defoe was a mercurial fellow, prolific writer and pamphleteer, feted or falling foul of both sides of the political divide. In his youth he fought with Monmouth and was one of only 29 men to receive a pardon from James II. He was no stranger to Bristol, initially as a glass tax inspector but also as a spy for the Dutch King, he made several repeat visits one of which coincided with Selkirk's stay in the city. He was known as 'a Sunday gentleman', only going out onto the streets on a Sunday when he could avoid his creditors. Never one to share his glory, Daniel Defoe always denied ever meeting Selkirk and was not impressed by the writings of Dampier or Rogers either, dismissing them both at the end of his life as *illiterate sailors*. In Rogers' case this may have been because of his books editor, George Ridpath, who had helped trigger Defoe's arrest in 1713 for high treason. Despite the denials, Dampier's descriptions of places and climates were definitely 'borrowed' for use in *Robinson Crusoe*. During his long life Defoe never left the British mainland.

Jonathon Swift published *Gulliver's Travels* in 1726 as a reaction to Defoe's classic and he never had a problem giving Dampier credit. In the opening passages of *Gulliver's Travels* he proclaims Dampier as Gulliver's cousin and has Gulliver set out on his adventure from Bristol in the good ship *Antelope*. Later on Bristol publisher Joseph Cottle bought Samuel Taylor Coleridge's *The Rime of the Ancient Mariner* in 1798 for 30 guineas and this epoch making ballad also drew on Bristol's Adventurers – Thomas James' arctic solitude and the exploits of one of Rogers' crew who failed to rendezvous on the Galapagos Islands. The latter was enslaved by the Spanish and couldn't get home for more than 15 years.

Another book spawned by a Bristol Adventurer was William Williams' *Journal of Llewellin Penrose, a Seaman,* first published in 1815. Many claim it to be the first American novel, but perhaps more notably it was the inspiration for Edgar Allan Poe's *The Gold Bug (or Beetle)* and through this, Robert Louis Stevenson's *Treasure Island.* The book concerns a castaway, named after Williams' Pennsylvania shipbuilding friends the Penroses who, with a nod to Crusoe, spends 27 years of his life amongst the Moskito and Carib tribes where he falls in love and has many an adventure.

World literature owes it a debt because Penrose's Journal is the first book that features an encrypted map, leading the way to buried pirate treasure, but if it wasn't for a Bristol classical scholar, Mr Thomas Eagles, the story would never have seen the light of day. Eagles had been approached in the street by an elderly vagabond clearly down on his luck but with a manner that betrayed a certain air of cultivation. He wanted access to St Peter's Hospital to see out his days. Eagles immediately managed to get what turned out to be a dying artist, author and American adventurer a berth in the Merchant Seaman's Almshouse in King Street.

The man was William Williams, son of a seafarer and born in Bristol in 1727. At a young age he left the city to become a painter in Britain's booming colonies of North America. He travelled extensively, spending a couple of years in Central America with the Moskito Indians and mixing with other native tribes, leading a full and eventful life. He is even credited as being one of Benjamin West's teachers, the American artist who became the second president of the Royal Academy (one of his famous paintings is 'The Treaty of Penn with the Indians'). His sons were lost in the Battle of Bunker Hill in 1775 and by the time he got back to Bristol he had no family left.

Once in his new home, Williams recovered a little and became firm friends with Eagles. The two enjoyed one another's company and Williams was a frequent visitor to the Eagles household, where the family revelled in his traveller's tales and discussions about art and literature.

He died in 1791, leaving all his worldly possessions to the person who gave him solace, Thomas Eagles; these included two manuscripts *Lives of the Painters* and another *The Journal of Llewellin Penrose, a Seaman.* On reading the latter manuscript, Lord Byron said *"Penrose is most amusing. I have never read so much of a book at one sitting in my life. He kept me up half the night, and made me dream of him the other half. It has all the air of truth, and is most entertaining and interesting in every point of view."*

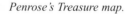

Penrose's Treasure map.

Thomas Eagles himself died in 1812, and it was his son, the Reverend John Eagles – 'Themaninthemoon' and author of *FelixFarley's Rymes, Latin and English* who exposed abuses in some of Bristol's public bodies – who got it published, slightly sanitized but with the proposed addition of illustrations by two of Bristol's finest ever artists, Nicholas Pocock and Edward Bird. Not many of these made it into the final book but the originals survived and have recently been acquired by the National Maritime Museum.

The novel that makes the most of Bristol's involvement with Pirates and Privateers is Robert Louis Stevenson's *Treasure Island,* written in the 1880s and firmly establishing Bristol as the home port for its ensuing adventure. Stevenson had the *Hispaniola* set sail from here, leaving behind Long John Silver's mulatto wife and his pub, the Spy-Glass Inn. At the time of the book's writing, RLS was in the company of classical Bristol scholar John Addington Symonds of Clifton Hill House, and he was surely a little responsible for the Scot setting part of his classic in Bristol. Stevenson freely acknowledged his 'borrowings' for *Treasure Island:* - the opening inn scene used Washington Irving's *Tales of a Traveller*, the parrot from Defoe's *Robinson Crusoe* and the encrypted map and pointing skeleton from Poe's *The Gold Bug*. If you go on the web to study Poe however, his debt to Williams isn't mentioned at all.

And the same is true of Bristol, where there is no acknowledgement to the debt that the city owes to its great Pirates and Privateers, let alone to their great literary connections, which is why the Long John Silver Trust came about. The aim of this registered charity is to recognise Bristol's maritime past, "Warts and all", and use the great literature that the city has inspired to enhance people's understanding. Blackbeard and Rogers, Dover and Dampier, none of these people were saints but their stories need to be told and what better way than with a 'Bristol Treasure Island Trail' – from Bristol's most historic street, King Street, to the new Museum of Bristol?

William Dampier was one of the most influential explorers of the 17th century. He was a swashbuckling naturalist whose contribution to navigation, science and literature was incredibly far reaching. His early life echoed that of Henry Morgan's and later on his extraordinary achievements predated those of James Cook and Charles Darwin. Born into a farming family in East Coker, Somerset, in 1651, he was the second of six children. Apprenticed at eighteen he became a seaman in Weymouth. Before long he found himself involved in the third Anglo-Dutch war of 1673 showing early signs of his future potential by making studies of prevailing winds during his first extended voyage. Young William then travelled to London but couldn't settle, leaving in 1674 to work on a Jamaican sugar plantation for a life little better than slavery. After falling out with the plantation manager he ran away and ended up in the Bay of Campeche to become a log wooder (felling precious timber that produced a red or purple dye, much coveted in Europe).

Here in the Caribbean swamps, Dampier found himself alongside some of Morgan's former pirates and buccaneers or 'Baymen' where he became one himself; as a faithful keeper of a journal he was later able to give a vivid account of their wild behaviour. It was also here that he got into the habit of making general observations of the world around him, a natural naturalist if you like. Buccaneers originated in the Caribbean, firstly on Hispaniola and then Tortuga. The term buccaneer derives from the French *boucanier* meaning people who smoked or cured strips of meat on a frame of green stick called

William Dampier

boucan, over a slow fire fed by animal bones and strips of hide. These were sold in bundles of 100 strips for 6 pieces of eight and were ideal for long voyages, keeping for weeks and softened in salt water to make them edible. Buccaneer lifestyle appealed to him and rather than fell lumber, Dampier joined in with their raids on Mexican coastal towns, ending up with a small fortune to his name.

Ever restless though, he returned to England in 1678 where he married Judith, a duchess's maid. Within a few months he told his wife he was off on a short trading trip to Jamaica, never thinking he would be away on an epic 12 year journey around the world that would make him famous. Instead of rejoining the log cutters, he sold his trade goods, bought a small estate in Dorset from a trader, sent the deeds home to his wife and then set sail from Port Royal to trade with the Moskito Indians. These indigenous Native Americans lived in a very inhospitable coastal region of the American mainland adjacent to the Caribbean, now part of the Nicaraguan coastline. After many bad encounters with the Spanish the Indians hated them with a passion and readily formed allegiances with the English, pirate or not. They were expert fisherman, easily capable of spearing anything in the sea and many a British seamen valued their contributions on board ship, reckoning rightly that they'd never go hungry.

It was on this trip that Dampier joined a multi-national buccaneering fleet under two more ex-Morgan men, Bartholomew Sharp and John Coxon, where they attacked Spanish held Portobello, Dampier receiving 100 pieces of eight for his part. After many escapades, including raiding Panama and crossing the Isthmus twice, he tried to settle in Virginia where he made one of his famous observations whilst removing an exotic worm which had become lodged in his leg. In 1683, ever the rover, Dampier then went on a piratical voyage with Captain John Cook. They crossed the Atlantic to the coast of West Africa and captured a Danish slaving vessel, *lovely ship, very fit for a long voyage*. She was also carrying 60 female African slaves and was renamed *The Bachelors Delight*. The fate of the Africans is not recorded; against William's wishes they rounded Cape Horn to enter the South Seas.

Dampier visited Juan Fernandez Island for the first time and they rescued a Moskito castaway, 'Will', who had been there *for above three years*. The reunion between this man and his countryman from the *Delight* touched them all. They resumed their quest for Spanish plunder up and down the Pacific coast of South America and despite now being led by Edward Davis they still met with hardly any success. Davis allowed Dampier to make naturalist's notes on the various places they visited, most notably the Galapagos Islands. In his frustration, Dampier left the *Delight* and took a berth on the *Cygnet*, belonging to Captain Swan and in order to escape the Spanish, Swan took his ship across the perilous Pacific to try and find safety and other prizes. It was a very arduous voyage and the crew were starving by the time they landed at a Spanish 'Baiting' Island'.* Prior to this the crew had already eyed up Swan for the pot, leading him to remark that Dampier would have made a poor meal, due to his lean and spare appearance.

In the Philippines, Swan and 40 of his crew mates were abandoned after a quarrel and the *Cygnet* sailed on trying to trade or plunder, Dampier stayed with the ship after it was taken over by Captain John Read. Dampier eventually managed to escape and after many more adventures got home with his slave, Jeoly, a man tattooed all over except for his face and hands. He was his only 'asset' apart from his journals. Jeoly's story is hugely sad; his party had been captured and enslaved after travelling to a nearby island and blown off course, they were seized by fishermen, looted and sold. Dampier came across him a couple of times before ending up with a half share in both him and his mother. When they both became sick in Bencouli (an English trading factory near Sumatra), Dampier nursed them. Unfortunately, Jeoly's mother died leaving him to accompany the buccaneer back to England after being promised that he would be returned home one day to freedom. When they turned up in London in 1691

* Supply base

50

Dampier had an awkward reunion with his wife and was then 'swindled' out of the services of Jeoly by some 'rooks'*. Jeoly went on to become a star exhibit in freak shows billed as 'The Painted Prince' and after much abuse he ended up alone, in a strange foreign land, dying of smallpox in Oxford. Jeoly may have been the template for Crusoe's Man Friday.

Although Dampier's achievements were great and varied, the fame he sought still alluded him, and it took him over five years to get his experiences published. After two years waiting for publication he went back to sea again and as usual, became embroiled in yet another momentous chapter in England's history, this time off the coast of Spain. A fleet had been assembled to attack French possessions in the West Indies, but due to lack of pay there was a mutiny during which the infamous Henry Avery seized the flagship for piratical purposes. Although he did not get involved, this incident was to dog Dampier in later years.

HMS Roebuck foundering off Ascension I.

In 1697 Dampier finally managed to get his manuscript published, and *A New Voyage Round the World* shot him from obscurity to celebrity in an instant. In the book Dampier mentions Rogers' father, another Captain Rogers who he called his *ingenious* friend, after corresponding with him on matters ranging from Hippopotamus in the River Natal to trade winds from the Cape of Good Hope to the Red Sea. All sorts of people were now interested in him, not least the fledgling Royal Society who had among their leading lights such people as Robert Hooke, Hans Sloane and Edmund Halley. This led to an invitation for Dampier to address the Society, where he shared his knowledge of winds, seas, tides and

* Rogues

currents to great acclaim.

Official recognition of his contributions followed in 1699 when he was given the command of *HMS Roebuck*, to explore Australia and the East Indies. However, Dampier was a poor leader of men and the transition from buccaneer to naval captain led to his court martial in 1702 on a charge of brutality. Successfully navigating all the way to Shark Bay in Australia, Dampier was within an ace of finding the elusive eastern seaboard. However, his ship was in terrible condition, and on his homeward voyage, rotten and worm eaten, it finally sank off Ascension Island in February 1701 – Dampier and his crew were rescued by the *Canterbury,* and he was home by August. Throughout his adventures, Dampier's papers and charts survived by his usual expedient of sealing them in bamboo tubes.

During the court martial, Dampier thought he was going to end up like Captain Kidd, whose tarred body was still hanging from a gibbet nearby in Execution Dock. He was finally fined three years wages and declared *not a fit person* to command a naval vessel, although this didn't stop him publishing a new book *A Voyage to New Holland* (Australia) in early 1703. Within a few months Dampier's powerful friends had enabled him to get another possibly lucrative privateering command against the Spanish, backed by a consortium led by Bristol merchant Thomas Estcourt. The mission was to seize the Spanish Atlantic Treasure Fleet and, if that failed, to round the Horn into the Pacific and attack a Manila Galleon.

Dampier commanded the *St George* and Charles Pickering the *Cinque Ports* galley and they set sail in autumn 1703. After a quarrelsome start several crew deserted at the Cape Verde islands. Pickering died and his young first lieutenant, Thomas Stradling, took command. Alexander Selkirk, a cantankerous seaman from Fife was appointed quartermaster. Seeming to forget about the Atlantic Fleet, they headed for the Pacific and rendezvoused on Juan Fernandez Island in February 1704. The ensuing harassment of the enemy turned into farce. Whilst attacking a French ship Dampier hid behind a mattress and later, when they captured a Spanish prize, let her go away without a thorough search. Both crews were unhappy and, against their owner's orders, split up some of their spoils and went their separate ways.

The leaking *Cinque Ports* went back to Juan Fernandez and Stradling completely fell out with Selkirk, this time leaving him behind. Selkirk's fears about the ship's safety were proved accurate though, as she sank soon afterwards leaving only eight survivors (including Stradling). After more mutinous and desperate encounters, Dampier and his remaining crew, just 27 by the end, left the worm-eaten ship *St George* and transferred to a captured Spanish brigantine. He once again crossed the Pacific and limped home after being away 3 years, his second circumnavigation.

By the end of 1707, apart from his navigational skills, his reputation was in tatters. Litigation was imminent but as some of the original Bristol backers wanted another 'go' at a treasure galleon they spirited him away. He managed to get the backing of some members of Bristol Corporation and other prominent Bristol merchants for a voyage that included a 'promising young captain', Woodes Rogers. As a family friend Woodes Rogers asked for Dampier to be the navigator and in the main this worked out very well, although they almost froze to death when he took them too far south whilst rounding Cape Horn. They then overshot Juan Fernandez Island but of course those were the days of poor charts and no accurate way of determining longitude. Even though the voyage was immensely successful, on Dampier's return in 1712 he was embroiled in litigation for his failures on the previous voyage. Diseased and weak in body, he died owing £2,000 in 1715, the most influential buccaneer ever.

Alexander Selkirk was born in Nether Largo in Fife, Scotland. The seventh son of a family of cobblers, he ran away from home at 15 after being charged with *undecent behaviour.* Apparently he *passed water* in church, and instead of coming to terms with his crime, he simply ran away, a pattern of action that he was to repeat throughout his life. He went to Leith and became a seaman, very soon learning the tricks of his trade; he became a true sailor, good enough to join the ill-fated Darien expedition of 1698 just three years later.

This was Scotland's attempt at becoming a colonial power and they cunningly chose a part of Central America which was only 40 miles wide, potentially giving Scotland control of trade between the Atlantic and the Pacific. Disease, starvation - they asked the English in Jamaica for help, but none was forthcoming, and then an attack by the Spanish ended the venture. Of the 1200 colonialists sent out, less than 300 returned. The main adviser for the mission was Lionel Wafer, a former colleague of Dampier's. One far reaching consequence of the campaign was that it nearly bankrupted Scotland and paved the way for union with England in 1707, much helped by the 'behind the scenes' machinations of one Daniel Defoe.

Now a mariner and man of the world, Selkirk returned home in 1701 only to violently fall out with his family. This time he accepted his punishment and promised *amendment,* but promptly went to sea again, rising to the rank of quartermaster after he joined the *Cinque Ports* galley on its ill-fated expedition with the *St George* in 1703 and a complete disaster. Dampier had huge problems leading the men, and was often accused of being drunk and violent for long periods of time. When the opportunity arose to take prizes, bad leadership led them to escape, especially one of the Manila galleons, where they attacked from completely the wrong direction, fuelling yet more dissention amongst the crew.

When Stradling took command of the *Cinque Ports* he was two years younger than Selkirk and this probably contributed to their strained relationship. It was the condition of the ship's hull that really concerned Selkirk however and it was his arguments about their leaky state that led to his abandonment. He later found out that he was vindicated because the ship soon sank. As the ramifications of marooning dawned on Selkirk he made an appeal to Stradling for clemency but Stradling's response was callous, instructing the crew to row away from the island. Selkirk never forgave Dampier for not sheathing the ships for protection against the worms before sailing. By this time the *St George* and the *Cinque Ports* were no longer in consort, so Dampier was unaware of Selkirk's plight. Alexander had been left with the following: - two day's supply of food, his sea chest containing clothes and bedding, a flintlock, powder and bullets, hatchet, knife and kettle, bible, mathematical instruments and books.

After being marooned on the remote Juan Fernandez Island Selkirk had over four years to dwell upon his bad luck. It's hard to imagine what nightmares and hardships he must have endured, living on goats, crayfish and seals. Alexander was so fast at chasing goats that on his rescue, he demonstrated how he could outrun Rogers' Bristol bulldog. Some of his marked goats (he nicked them on their ears) were discovered over thirty years later by Lord Anson's expedition. Selkirk was also persistently annoyed by rats. They nibbled at him during the night, so he solved the problem by training cats to sleep around his cot. Not content with this he then trained them to 'dance' with him. After Selkirk's rescue, Woodes Rogers famously described him *as a man cloth'd in Goat-skins, who looked wilder than the first owners of them.* Selkirk had trouble speaking *for want of use* (not because of his Scottish accent!) and *he seemed to speak his words by halves.* Rogers called him the Governor of the Island and its Absolute Monarch and also noted his 'close' relationship to his cloven hoofed friends. Dampier recommended Selkirk, and he was appointed Second Mate on the *Duke.*

Because of his enforced celibacy, Rogers had Selkirk searching the ladies for their heavy gold chains at Guayaquil.

Rogers and Selkirk got on well and, on reaching Bristol after the voyage, Selkirk stayed around hoping to get a berth on a new expedition for the South Seas Company that Woodes Rogers was trying to bring to fruition, staying initially in Rogers' house at 19 Queen Square. During this time Selkirk wrote a deposition against Dampier for his role in the *St George* fiasco. His stay in Bristol lasted nearly two years until he once again fell foul of the authorities and ran away after being charged with attacking a fellow sailor, Richard Nettle, in 1713 in the parish of St Stephen's.

On the return of Rogers' expedition, two books came out in quick succession that propelled Selkirk's status to stellar heights, and *A Cruising Voyage Round the World* by Woodes Rogers himself, became an international best seller. Selkirk enjoyed his celebrity, and it is recorded that he often paraded around the streets of Bristol in his goat skins, meeting with Bristol's *convivial wits* including Defoe, in the Star Inn – which was built above Bristol Castle's dungeon keep. Although Defoe denied ever meeting him, several local people swore affidavits to the effect that the famous writer had taken Selkirk's papers and used them for his masterpiece, *Robinson Crusoe*, reputedly the first ever novel in English. Selkirk went back to Largo a wealthy man, with £800 from his share of the Manila galleon and copies of all the books that had been written about him. He built a cave in his father's garden and tried to settle, marrying a local girl Sophia Bruce after they eloped to London, but it didn't work out. He enlisted in the navy and served initially on *HMS Enterprise* as mate and then *HMS Weymouth* as first mate. Before going on his last voyage he 'married' again, leading to all sorts of problems for his first wife.

Selkirk's final mission was to protect Britain's slaving interests in West Africa, at that time being attacked by pirates led by 'Black Bart' Roberts. *HMS Weymouth* and *HMS Swallow* were sailing together to try and suppress Roberts' pirate gang, which was by now the largest the world had ever known, after a string of staggeringly successful escapades. Selkirk's ship was stricken by illness and the prototype for Robinson Crusoe, The Island Monarch himself, died of disease on 13th December 1721. Within three months *Weymouth's* sister ship, the *Swallow,* successfully attacked Black Bart and his pirates, promptly ending the pirates 'Golden Age'.

Thomas Dover was born on a Cotswolds farm in 1662 and was one of eight children of a Cavalier who fought

Ken Battersbury's painting of Dover meeting Selkirk for the first time. Researched by and portrayed in Glenside Hospital Museum.

with Prince Rupert during the Civil War. He studied medicine as a commoner at Oxford and graduated with a BA at the age of 22, following this by serving a clinical apprenticeship under the famous Dr Sydenham who saved his life with a radical treatment after he contracted small pox. After marrying and inheriting the family farm he moved to Bristol where he became one of the city's few practitioners, coming to notice in 1695 by being the first to offer his services free of charge to the poor of St Peters Hospital.

By the turn of the century he decided to go to sea, on hearing of the huge profits some Bristol's merchants were making from their new involvement into the Trans-Atlantic Slave Trade he joined Bristol's near sixty strong African fleet that had mushroomed since 1698. From 1701 to 1707 he made several 'Triangular' trades, initially as a doctor but then as a sea captain, proving that he was an able man. This may have been where he earned the sobriquet 'Cap'n Quicksilver' – later to be the 'Quicksilver Doctor' – for the then dangerous treatment of VD. "One night with Venus, a week with Mercury" was the old saying in sailor parlance.

He made so much money that when Dampier came to Bristol to promote a voyage to take a Spanish Treasure Ship he became the second highest investor, earning the right to go on the voyage as second captain and to protect his fellow investor's interests. As ever, this didn't preclude him looking after his own interests; when the captured *Marquis* came up for sale in Java, he sold it to one Captain Opie. Rogers described this transaction as an *extraordinary bargain*. Opie ended up as Dover's son-in-law. The successful cruise took three years. The original shareholders should have received £98,650 and the crews £49,325, but after litigation and much *profligation* (which particularly incensed Thomas Goldney) they received only £50,109. However, they still doubled their money. The crew were less fortunate; 'Smart Money'* was paid to the disabled and wounded, but many of the survivors were press ganged and did not receive their full pay for another three years.

The enormous tussle with the East India Company on the successful adventurers return brought Dover to the attention of the great and the good of London and after the affair was settled he was offered the plum job of President at Buenos Aires for the newly formed South Seas Company on a salary of £1,000 per annum. *The Treaty of Utrecht* laid down certain conditions for British dealings in the Americas and Dover started breaking them soon after his arrival by private trading, possibly dabbling in the slave trade yet again, ultimately leading to his dismissal in 1716.

The Doctor had invested most of the proceeds of his

* *A Priority payment.*

cruising voyage into the South Seas Company and when it crashed in 1720 he lost every penny, forcing him to take up medicine once again as a more active practitioner. The future first British Prime Minister, Sir Robert Walpole managed to sell his shares just in time - at a considerable profit... Dover didn't but was an accomplished medical man so when another smallpox epidemic broke out he treated many well connected people successfully. As ever he couldn't resist condemning his less able peers and this led to a lot of professional rivalry.

His defiant nature led his practice to dwindle and seven years on his debts from the South Sea Bubble crash were still around his neck, leading him to take semi-retirement back in Gloucestershire, with no wife, home or fortune. He quietly came back into vogue, first in the Cotswolds, then Bristol and finally London again. In 1734 he wrote a best selling book *The Ancient Physicians Legacy,* featuring his avocation of applying mercury and the recipe for his famous Powder that contained opiates which went on

Lying in wait to attack Guayaquil, most of Rogers' men contracted swamp fever.

to be used for another 200 years. He died at the age of 80, still attacking the College of Physicians and the Society of Apothecaries.

According to an article by D.N.Phear in 1954 *"Few medical men have lived more eventfully than Doctor Thomas Dover, the Bristol physician whose name is enshrined in Dover's Powder. Obstinate, boastful, and quarrelsome he was, but generous to the poor, devoted to his friends, and venturesome enough, at the age of forty-six, to sail on a voyage of plunder to the Spanish Main where he shared in the rescue of Robinson Crusoe."*

He was also a hero of Patrick O'Brian, the acclaimed late 20th Century writer who regarded him as the unsung hero of Woodes Rogers' epic voyage, giving him full credit for saving the lives of a large part of Rogers' crew once they had come down with swamp fever after the attack on Guayquil. He said as much in his excellent Aubery/Maturin series of historical novels, complementing the fact by portraying one of Dr Maturin's arch enemies as a Bristol Privateer – Maturin finally dispatching him in a duel.

Woodes Rogers' memory and his achievements don't seem to sit very easily with some modern day Bristolians, possibly clouded by the strong possibility that he dabbled with the slave trade. He wasn't however, one of the major players (to use modern parlance). He didn't set up slave stations or own plantations, but he didn't shy away from using anyone or anything to enable him to get on in life. His life was mercurial, his round the world circumnavigation and his two stints as the Governor of the Bahamas are well documented, but these are mere snapshots of a very full life. Although he was a resourceful man, a good leader, magnificent seamen and brave, he had, like the great Marlborough of this period, a fair few detractors.

The third generation to carry the Woodes Rogers name, the family was originally from Poole in Dorset, where the Rogers' were prominent citizens. Several had even been mayors in the town during the reign of Elizabeth I. All of them had strong maritime connections. It's not known whether Woodes was born in Bristol or not, but his father, a successful sea captain (who sailed the Atlantic and Indian Oceans) had moved to the port at around the time of Woodes Roger's birth in 1679. Rogers followed in his ancestors footsteps and became apprenticed in Bristol as a 'nautica' (sailor). Not much is known about his early career, and some say he commanded two privateers from 1705 to 1707 on cruises in the English Channel against the French threat, whilst others say he sustained losses when trading in the Newfoundland fisheries.

In January of 1705 he married Sarah Whetstone, daughter of Bristol Admiral Sir William Whetstone, also sharing an interest in the *Whetstone* galley slave ship with his father-in-law, which was captured by the French in early 1708. After marrying Sarah, his status in Bristol improved tremendously and he became both a Merchant Venturer and Freeman of the City. When William Dampier came to Bristol late in 1707 to drum up support for an expedition to seize a Manila treasure ship he found Rogers a willing and able accomplice; Rogers had already been fired by the recent success of French navy captain Beauchesne Gouin's efforts to trade in the South Seas, where he had made a fortune for himself and France.

Dampier singled Rogers out as showing great promise, both as an administrator and leader of men; he was duly made Commander of the venture which was being backed by leading members of Bristol Corporation who were keen to make good their losses at the hands of French privateers. The timing was perfect, it was at the height of the War of the Spanish Succession and Queen Anne had just relinquished the crown's right to a fifth of all the proceeds of prizes taken (in order to encourage British privateers). In all, Bristol issued 127 letters of marque during the war but British losses to French privateers amounted to over 3,600 merchant vessels.

The consortium was given its Letter of Marque enabling them to legitimately attack Spanish and French trade and

Left: A stained glass window of St. Wulfstan in Worcester Catherdral. The last Anglo-Saxon Bishop, Patron Saint of peasants and vegetarians. The first campaigner to abolish slavery in Bristol in the 11th century.

Right: The Tomb of William Canynge, a 15th century Bristol merchant. He built up the largest fleet of privately owned vessels in the kingdom, if not Europe; one of them the *Mary and John* was reputed to be over 800 tons, a massive ship in medieval times. His business interests were so extensive that it is said that Canning Town in London was named after him. He invested a large proportion of his money into developing St. Mary Redcliffe Church. William Canynge died in 1474.

Above: A memorial plaque in Bristol Cathedral to Richard Hakluyt, renaissance diplomat, sometime spy and famous geographer. He settled into Bristol's new Cathedral, the former Abbey of St. Augustine in the 16th century. He gathered together all the known accounts of voyages of discovery to use in his seminal work, *The Principal Navigations, Voyages, Traffiques and Discoveries of the English Nation.* He was the inspiration for many of Bristol's future voyages of discovery.

Right: Admiral Sir William Penn's memorial, armour and replica battle standards in St. Mary Redcliffe church, Bristol. He was one of the most successful admirals of the 17th century, taking Jamicia from the Spanish.

Above left: A stained glass window of Admiral Robert Blake in Bristol Cathedral. Born in Bridgwater he reorganised the Navy into an efficient force. He fought many successful battles against the Dutch and the Barbary Coast Pirates.

Above right. The 'Robinson Crusoe' Candlesticks in Bristol Cathedral donated by one of Woodes Rogers grateful backers.

Left: The Martin Pring memorial in St. Stephen's Church Bristol. He was one of England's foremost seafarers exploring both the North American Coast and the East Indies, paving the way for colonisation and trade. The memorial is a joy of vibrant colour and iconography depicting episodes of his life through the tools of his trade, from quadrants and mitres to shovels and picks, all supported by a delightful mermaid and merman. The church is his final resting place.

This plaque to Thomas Clarkson was unveiled by Richard Hart, a civil rights lawyer from Jamaica on the 1st. of May 2009 outside the Seven Stars pub, St. Thomas Lane, Bristol. The plaque was designed by Mike Baker on behalf of Bristol Radical History Group to mark the 200th Anniversary of the abolition of the Slave Trade in 2007. Thomas Clarkson was the pre-eminent ant-slavery campaigner of the 18th Century and came to the inn in 1787 to reseach the horrors of the Trade. Clarkson first showed that the seamen were being abused and in many cases losing their lives by being tricked and forced aboard the slave ships. He then demonstrated how badly the slaves themselves were being treated. In this he was helped greatly by Landlord Thompson of the Seven Stars, who at great personal risk introduced Clarkson to victims of the trade and to the haunts of the crimpers. This was a perrenial problem for the sailors who also tried to avoid the press gang, sometimes escaping up river to Crews Hole for sanctuary.

possessions; they invested £26,496 in the venture, not an insignificant sum for those days and Captain Woodes Rogers was appointed commander with, on Rogers' insistence, Dampier as pilot. Other notable members were Dr Thomas Dover and Carlton Vanburgh, brother of the famous architect who designed Blenheim Palace and Kingsweston House in Bristol. Vanburgh did not survive the cruise. Two ships were built and commissioned in Bristol, the *Duke* (thirty guns, 320 tons) and *Duchess* (twenty-six guns, 260 tons) and Rogers insisted on William Dampier as the navigator - despite his reputation being somewhat dented by recent events. Perhaps because of Dampier's previous experiences, the two ships had their hulls double sheathed for protection. The two frigates set sail from Bristol on 15th June 1708 and headed for Kinsale, near Cork in Ireland, where Woodes Rogers promptly set about changing half his crew.

According to Rogers the crew consisted for the most part of *Tinkers, Taylors, Hay-makers, Pedlars, Fiddlers, etc.,* and they even had a *wholesale oilman from London* as ships steward. The compliment was rounded off by the ships mascot, *a fine specimen of an English bull-dog.* Known locally as Bristol mastiffs these were very popular additions to long voyages from the ancient port. One of the supplies that they carried was 'red-streak cyder' – Pepys wrote that *seamen love their bellies above anything else* but Rogers was of the opinion that *good liquor to sailors is preferable to clothing.* After exploring the Falkland Islands the ships rounded Cape Horn and landed on the island of Juan Fernandez in the Pacific where they rescued Alexander Selkirk.

The expedition then went about its business of attacking Spanish trade and commerce in the South Seas. One of the most successful raids was on the rich Spanish possession of Guayaquil where the expedition tried to ransom the city. When this failed they attacked and apparently

Rogers' men, led by Selkirk, liberated the Spanish ladies of their gold chains in *a most genteel manner.* This attack made several of the crew ill through staying in the swampy estuary for too long, and Dr Dover did a superb job in saving as many as he could from fever. Just prior to this, when trying to board a French enemy ship, Woodes Rogers' younger brother John was killed. Within 24 hours the ship was captured and renamed the Marquis.

More adventures and many prizes later, Woodes Rogers managed to finally secure a Treasure Ship at the great personal cost of a bullet in the mouth which shattered his upper jaw and cost him many teeth. Whist gurgling blood

The 'Duke' engaging the ' Nuestra Senora de la Incarnacion Disenganio' at daybreak on 22nd December 1708.

he carried on the attack by writing down his commands. Then, despite being heavily outgunned, the party tried to attack an even bigger Treasure Ship, with Rogers receiving yet another injury, a huge wooden splinter in his heel. The largest cannon Rogers had at his disposal was a 24 pounder, and the shot just bounced off the sides of the bigger Treasure Ship. After this failure, the decision was made to sail for home by crossing the Pacific, stopping off at Batavia (Java) for Woodes Rogers to receive much needed surgery.

The captured Treasure Ship the *Nuestra Señora de la Encarnación y Desengaño* was renamed *The Batchelor,* after one of the voyages sponsors, Alderman Batchelor of Bristol (apparently not because of the *Bachelors Delight* – one of Dampier's former ships). There was a dispute over who would command her and Rogers managed to get Selkirk appointed master over the unpopular Dr Dover. They cruised on to South Africa where they waited for a convoy, essential to protect themselves from French privateers, to take them safely back home. The convoy happened to be Dutch and to avoid the French went north of the Shetlands to end up in Tetzel, prior to the final hop across to the Thames and so called safety in London. The East India Company was baying for Rogers' blood as he had foolishly dealt in arrack whilst in the East. This was a kind of spirit on which the East India Company had a monopoly.

Once home Rogers lost his home in Queen Square for a while and to try and raise some funds, and probably to state his side of events, he published a book based around his captain's log which proved to be a best seller and hugely influential. This wasn't the only book published about the voyage. His fellow captain, Cooke, also published one but it didn't get the critical acclaim or sales that Rogers' *A Cruising Voyage Round the World* did, it also benefited from the formerly secret Spanish maps of the South Seas taken by Rogers' expedition that were published within - these helped fuel the South Sea Bubble.

By 1718 Woodes Rogers was off on his next adventure, this time being made the first Royal Governor of the Bahamas. This was something of a poisoned chalice as the islands had become a pirates' republic, home to some of the most ferocious pirates ever. Our man was required to take their pardon or fight them. To aid him he had been given command of the 40 gun *Delicia* as his flagship, and in the beginning, a Royal Navy escort *HMS Rose.* Not only did he re-establish the colony for the British, he even managed to get the pardoned pirates to fight off the Spanish.

His main quest was initially successful. Nearly all of the pirates took the pardon including Blackbeard's old master Benjamin Hornigold who became firm friends with Rogers and ultimately one of his leading aides. Others weren't quite so obliging; the notorious Charles Vane broke out of New Providence on Rogers' arrival leading to charges of incompetence for the captain of the *Rose*. In a fit of temper this led to the hapless navy man getting a crack over the head from Woodes Rogers's pistol butt. Pirates that failed to take King George's pardon were dealt with harshly and there was a big show trial for several miscreants leading to a large public hanging. This was said to have been outside of the Governor's remit but it had the desired effect. When the Spanish tried to mount an attack to retake the Bahamas, Rogers managed to get over 400 of the former rabble rousers to join him in the defence of the islands.

Within a few years though, Rogers left Nassau after using up all of his own and his backers' money trying to make the colony succeed. He returned home destitute and his fortunes fluctuated again. Probably a stint in debtors prison being his lowest moment and having his family's portrait painted by the great William Hogarth in 1729, the highest. During this period he is mentioned in Johnson's *General History of ye Pyrates;* on a slaving expedition back to Batavia in the *Delicia,* Woodes Rogers calls in on the pirate island of Madagascar to find survivors of Avery's time (see the chapter Red Sea Rovers). Here he trades with them, exchanging goods for slaves, but when he discovers a plot to overcome his ship he promptly leaves, taking the slaves with him but leaving the pirates to their *dirty state of Royalty*. This voyage could have taken place before his first stint as Governor of the Bahamas.

Ten years before, some of Rogers' companions had accused him of leaving some of the Spanish treasure in Batavia, and it seems a funny coincidence that he chose-to go back there on a slaving voyage, bearing in mind that massive profits were to be had going the other way to the Americas! All this was prior to his final stint as Governor of the Bahamas in 1729, where he carried on with his colonial duties, setting up the island's first General Assembly and trying to attract more trade and people to the colony. Unsurprisingly, during these periods of gov-ernorship, Woodes Rogers made enemies and this may account for his mysterious death in 1732 when he was possibly poisoned. Just as mysteriously he has no corner of a foreign land, his grave is unknown.

In his home town of Bristol there's just a Civic Society blue plaque to mark the site of Woodes Rogers house in Queen Square, while in the Bahamas there are several reminders of him; his statue erected in the 1930s outside the Colonial Hilton Hotel in Nassau, plaques proclaiming his achievement in setting up the colony's first General Assembly and where latter day cruise ships moor up, a road named after him, 'Woodes Rogers Walk'. This is quite ironic as after his encounter with the second Spanish Treasure ship, where one of his heels was sliced off by a large wooden splinter – he walked with a limp.

This picture by the great William Hogarth comes from his early "Conversation Pieces" series of paintings. It depicts Woodes Rogers with his daughter Sarah and his son William along with iconography from Rogers' life- a globe, a Privateer and a portion of the defensive wall of Fort Nassau. The painting was completed in 1729 just prior to Rogers' final, second, stint as Governor of the Bahamas. It now resides in storage at the National Maritime Museum in Greenwich; surely this picture should be on display in Bristol.

Red Sea Rovers –the Pirate Round

The Red Sea first became a target for European pirates in the late 17th Century when a former wealthy Jamaican plantation owners' son, on the run for murder, set up a trading fort on the island of St Mary's just off Madagascar. His name was Adam Baldridge, and he more or less set the island up to become the base for European pirating activities throughout the Indian Ocean. He made a fortune selling on commodities brought over from America's fledgling colonies, which were already disgruntled at the way they were taxed. Wine, he could sell for fifteen times what it cost in New York and two shillings worth of rum was sold for three pounds a gallon. In the background he was supported by corrupt governors ranging from Bermuda to Boston.

One fellow who made it good, or even better, through this pirate brokering was Sir William Phips, an impoverished American born son of a Bristol gunsmith. In his youth he came up with the great idea of salvaging treasure from wrecked Spanish ships, and with the backing of King Charles II and his son James II - who shared in the loot, he became very wealthy. As a reward he received a knighthood and governorship of the huge Massachusetts Bay Colony, called New England today.

The pirate colony's fortunes ebbed and flowed, but it was prominent for about 30 years from 1690. During this period it flourished for a while under the name of 'Libertilia' when a former French privateer called Captain Mission, with his mentor Father Caraccioli, tried to set up a socialist utopia.

Three of the most sensational pirates/privateers came from this period and the following each have a place in this history.

Captain Tew's flag.

Thomas Tew was a Rhode Island man who came to prominence in the 1680s where he was a sea rover based in Jamaica. By late 1692 he bought a privateering commission from Isaac Richier the lieutenant governor of Bermuda. The aim of this commission was to attack a French slaving station on the river Gambia in West Africa and to do it Tew had bought a share of an eight gun sloop named the *Amity*.

They set sail for Africa in consort with another sloop under the command of George Dew, but when a storm badly damaged the ship's mast Dew turned back and Tew found himself and sixty crew on their own. He then had a rethink and urged his men to abandon their original quest and aim for the rich pickings of the Indian Ocean. To persuade his men Tew said to them, (it would) "lead them to a life of plenty, in which they might pass the rest of their days; that one bold push would do their business, and they might return home, not only without danger, but even with reputation". Apparently his men' to a man replied, "A gold chain or a wooden leg, we will stand by you". Against orders they rounded the Cape of Good Hope and started searching for prey, enemy or neutral. In July 1693 they came across one the Great Mogul's rich merchant ships heading for the Red Sea, laden with gold and silver, coffers of gems and 'elephants teeth' – as well as spices and silks. They gave it a fusillade and despite having 300 soldiers on board, took it without the loss of a single man.

They found safe haven in Baldridge's fortress on St Mary's and divided up the spoils. Some of Tew's crew decided to stay with him but the rest wanted to quit while they were ahead. Apparently Tew found time to bolster Mission's utopia on Madagascar with some liberated slaves but when the Portuguese attacked, killing Caraccioli, Tew and Mission took their leave. Sailing in consort back to Rhode Island, Mission's heavily laden treasure ship capsized, losing all hands and Tew was left to journey home alone with his men and their valuables. In the main he received a hero's welcome, but he had to return to Bermuda to pay off his original backers. He rewarded them with fourteen times their original stake.

Tew was home by April 1694 and enjoyed being feted for a while, but the lure of easy pickings and yet more wealth proved too great; when he advertised for crewmen for another voyage to the Red Sea he was overwhelmed with landsmen deserting their posts and trying to sign up. After only seven months, Tew was ready to embark again on his sloop the *Amity,* and after uncovering some stowaways, he crossed the Atlantic and rounded Africa aiming once again for the safe haven of Madagascar. Here he encountered Avery and his mutineers and after mistaking them for the Royal Navy, agreed to team up. They sailed in consort and encountered their prey in September 1695 but this time the Mogul's ship responded differently and put up a fight with Tew getting shot in his stomach. Using his hand to keep his bowels from spilling out, he tried to fight on until weakness overcame him and he dropped dead, affecting the resolve of his men, and putting them into the hands of Avery and his henchmen.

Captain Avery's flag.

Henry Avery (Evry, Benjamin Bridgeman or Long Ben) was a Devonian and stole a ship in 1694 that led to one of the greatest acts of piracy ever executed. After an unimpressive career in the Royal Navy, he'd been stationed off the Spanish coast for over a year without pay on board *HMS Charles.* He was First Officer to Captain Gibson. Other ships in the flotilla were the *Seventh Son, Dove* galley (with Dampier on board) and *James II,* two of which, according to Captain Johnson, were Bristol privateers. With other disgruntled members of her crew Avery mutinied and led them away, renaming the ship the *Fancy,* this had been made easier by the fact that the *Charles'* captain *was in his cups* * everyday.

This episode caused Dampier great problems later on as during his court martial after losing *HMS Roebuck;* he was accused of knowing Avery from his buccaneering Campeche days, and somehow being involved in the mutiny. Dampier was indeed angry about the lack of pay at the time and the accusations after, but he didn't take part in Avery's adventure. The whole situation was a strange twist in the fortunes of war. At one time in league with the French, the Spanish had changed their minds and become allies of William III of England. The force had been assembled initially to attack French interests in the Caribbean, but the Spanish became wary of the venture and after Avery's mutiny the proposal was dropped.

After slipping quietly away from Corunna, the *Charles'* captain sobered up, only to be confronted by Avery who gave him two options, "If you have a mind to make one of us, we will receive you, and if you'll turn sober, and mind your business, perhaps in time I may make you one of my lieutenants. If not, here's a boat alongside, and you shall be set ashore." Captain Gibson accepted the last offer with alacrity and made off with just five or six others who also wanted to avoid going 'on the account'**. Before any organised pursuit could be mounted, Avery and his men raced away, avoiding all and sundry before rounding the Cape of Good Hope and onward to his final destination of Madagascar.

Madagascar is a large island lying off the East African coast in the Indian Ocean and at that time was ignored by the European powers, but not by pirates who found it a

* Inebriated
**Signing pirate articles (contract)

61

perfect haunt with its abundant supplies of food and water. As the *Fancy* swung into the north-eastern part of the island they found two sloops at anchor, whose crews on being spotted immediately ran into the hinterland, mistaking the visitors as being from the authorities. On realising their mistake the sloop's crew readily agreed to join Henry and his men on their quest for a prize and what a prize they had in mind, none other than one of the Great Mogul's ships. One of the sloop's captains was Thomas Tew, who already had experience of taking such a prize, but now with a large frigate to help him and his comrades well armed, their chances of success had been helped greatly.

While not apparently interested in Madagascar, the European powers were definitely interested in mighty India and most of them had set up trading stations there, keen to curry the Mogul's favour. The Grand Mogul himself, Aurangzeb, was fabulously wealthy with a massive standing army and, as goes along with such status, huge power and influence. Avery wasted no time and sailed in consort with the two sloops to the mouth of the River Indus off the Bombay coast, and on 8th September 1695 a sail was spotted and in sight came the *Ganj-i-sawai*, nicknamed the Gunsway, packed with members of the Mogul's court, pilgrims for Mecca and fabulous riches in the form of diamonds and silk, gold and silver.

On seeing the Mogul's colours, Avery cannonaded her from a distance while the two sloops went into action, one on the victims bow and one on her quarter where…. *they 'clapt' her on board and entered her, upon which she immediately struck her colours and yielded.* The pirates then went into a frenzy of murder, torture, raping and pillaging, where even the Mogul's favourite niece was abused, much to his huge fury. Some of his concubines took their own lives rather than be subject to more harsh treatment. The plunder was said to be in the region of over £200,000 - a massive amount for those days. After the glut of excess, Avery and his pirates parted from the Mogul's ship, taking all of the treasure and some of the women, heading for the safety of Reunion to divvy up the spoils. On the way, Avery showed another side to his devious character by tricking the crews of the two sloops into placing their spoils aboard the *Fancy* for safe keeping. Needless to say, as soon as there was a favourable wind, they lost their consort and their booty.

The outcry from this dastardly action rang around the corridors of power throughout Europe and the East. With the Mogul being immediately informed that the pirates were English, it instantly compromised the position of the East India Company. He declared he would send a mighty army with fire and sword to drive the English from all of their settlements on the Indian coast. By degrees the Company managed to pacify him by promising to take the robbers and deliver them into his hands, hence the secret plot formed by Captain Kidd and his well connected London backers to become a Pirate Hunter. This was in the future though and Avery made every effort to escape the wrath that was brewing by heading immediately around the Cape of Good Hope and on to safety in the Caribbean. Things went well; he was able to sell the *Fancy* and divide up the spoils but in so doing he made a crucial error, he kept his share in diamonds and with the furore generated, these were the hardest of all to dispose of.

The crew sensibly split up and scattered to the four corners, a few that stayed together got apprehended, but Avery gingerly made his way back to Britain via Boston and Ireland, coming to rest finally in Bideford. It was here he made his final mistake, he decided to trust his diamonds and remaining affects with some Bristol merchants. After only receiving a small supply of money in exchange for his worldly goods he decided to go to

Bristol to confront them. Here he received a shocking repulse; if he said anything of the matter they would 'discover' him. According to Johnson again…. *our merchants were as good pirates at land as he was at sea.*

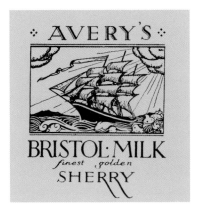

He returned to Bideford to finish his days in a life of beggary, so poor he couldn't afford a coffin. On the stage he became famous as the hero of *The Successful Pyrate* and in a sea shanty *The Ballad of Long Ben.* The celebrated Bristol firm of wine merchants 'Avery's' are said to be descended from him.

William Kidd's name will forever be associated with piracy whether he intended it to be or not, and whatever is said about him he paid the ultimate price – dangling from the end of a rope. It was his political masters' fall from grace that determined his fate more than his own actions, a cautionary tale for anyone interested in politics. He was a brave man and a decent leader, finally outwitted by cunning, ruthless people both at sea and on land.

Born in Dundee and fatherless by the age of five, he went to sea and ended up in the Caribbean, associating with miscreants all looking for their main chance. Writer A.P.Thornton called it *a cauldron where the bad blood of Europe boiled at will.* In 1689, at the age of 35, he rose to fame as a privateer defending English possessions for General Christopher Codrington against the mighty privateer Admiral Du Casse, the French equivalent of Henry Morgan. Codrington had massive sugar plantations on Barbados and for his loyal service to the Crown he had been bequeathed the island of Barbuda which later found notoriety as a kind of human stud farm for the supply of slaves. He also acquired a massive country seat just north of Bristol at Doddington where his family lavished their wealth onto a huge estate covering a large chunk of South Gloucestershire.

Ironically, Kidd was one of eight 'English' who had signed up for the Frenchman's privateering mission against the carcass of Spanish interests that the Dutch, French and English were picking over. It was on a mission against the Dutch that news came through that Dutch William had become King of England and immediately declared war on France. Du Casse made a judgement that Kidd and his colleagues were more interested in profit than patriotism – but he was wrong. During a French attack against St Kitts, a prosperous island remarkably shared by both the English and French, Kidd's men were left aboard the *Sainte Rose* with only a token number of Frenchmen. On Kidd's command the English slit the throats of their hosts and took the ship, sailing immediately to the aid of Codrington on Nevis. There the captured vessel was renamed the *Blessed William* with Kidd and his cronies hailed as heroes, the only salvation the

English defenders had enjoyed for months.

St Kitts was evacuated and Antigua became the next English stronghold. The marauding French stalled allowing Codrington to take stock. The *Blessed William*, now with Kidd as captain, was sent to Barbados to get men and supplies and on his return Kidd surprised a French brigantia and two sloops re-watering on the island of Dominique. He immediately took them all as prizes, auctioning them off on his victorious return to Antigua.

Kidd's fame spread and his crew was swelled by ever more desperadoes on the look out for a bit of success. Codrington's luck was changing and his small force was joined by a bigger English privateer the *Lion* commanded by Captain Hewetson – "scelerat cruel" or cruel scoundrel as the French called him - and now some form of defence could be maintained. Bolstered, the General decided to go on the offensive by attacking a soft French target, the sugar rich island of Mariegalante, aided by a group of French Huguenots who helped him with his plans.

In addition to the *Blessed William* and the *Lion,* Codrington added the 10 gun *Speedwell* under Captain Perry and rounded the fleet off with two troop sloops of his own, the *Barbados* and the *Hope,* all to be under the general command of Captain Hewetson. Just after Christmas 1689 they set sail to wreak havoc on the island of 1,000 souls. Captain Kidd's men received no pay for this duty but were rewarded by a share of the spoils. Mariegalante was taken easily by the English with a well worked plan; Hewetson led the land forces and Kidd the sea forces, chasing the French off into the hinterland. Codrington remarked on their return to Antigua that to some measure they had avenged the French victory at St Kitt's.

No sooner had they started spending their hard gotten gains when word reached them that another English force under Sir Timothy Thornhill had run into trouble attacking the French island of St Martin. Admiral Du Casse had them trapped and had raised the blood red flag – "La Jolie Rouge" anglicised to Jolly Roger – advising Thornhill's force that they would receive no quarter. Codrington immediately despatched Hewetson and Kidd to their aid and despite being outnumbered and outgunned they still gave a good account of themselves. Wily Du Casse pretended to retreat allowing the English to try and collect their beleaguered comrades only to reappear with an even larger fleet. The two sides exchanged broadsides again and again, but when the English tried to grapple the French and engage with hand to hand combat, the French thought better of it and retreated long enough for Thornhill's force to be rescued.

Battered, bruised and triumphant, Hewetson and Kidd led the remnants back to Antigua to receive another victor's welcome. Kidd's delight was short lived however as his former shipmates stole the *Blessed William* along with Kidd's personal fortune, some £2,000. One of the thieves was Robert Culliford, who had been with Kidd when they first took the *Blessed William* from the French. He would prove to be Kidd's nemesis for the rest of his life. One of the reasons Culliford and his cronies chose this course of action was that they had been made to swear 'Articles of War' before their last engagement. They disliked being subject to any kind of authority and returned to their buccaneering roots as soon as they were able.

Codrington gave Kidd another commission and he served under the General until the Royal Navy finally came late in 1690. Kidd had heard rumours about his *Blessed William* pirating up the North American coast and he was determined to follow and make amends for his losses. He set sail for New York and was immediately embroiled in local politics on his arrival. Corrupt Governor Leisler was refusing to give up his office and Kidd, now in charge of the 16 gun *Antigua* that Codrington had rewarded him with, used the privateer to secure his capture. Leisler's cause was not helped by the intelligence Kidd had learned about him making friends with his mutinous former shipmates.

Kidd rose in status and carried on privateering along the American seaboard where he met with a modicum of success. His biggest prize however was wedding a very young and attractive New York widow with whom he set about elevating their social position, buying a mansion and being feted in society. From this happy union they had a daughter. By 1695 Kidd still hankered after the sea and yet more status, sailing off to London to try and apply directly to War Secretary Lord Blathwayt for a Captain's commission in the Royal Navy.

As an aside, Blathwayt's country seat was adjacent to Codrington's just North East of Bristol at Dyrham, the site of a battle in AD577 between the West Saxons and the Romano-British Celts, which split the Celts forever.

Unfortunately for Kidd, Blathwayt was away in Holland with the homesick and depressed King (who had lost his beloved Queen Mary) but while in London Kidd fell in with a suspect New York merchant named Livingston who had concocted a deadly ruse. After Avery's pirating success Livingston wanted a piece of the action and cooked up a scheme revolving around Kidd becoming a 'pirate hunter' - to basically rob the robbers. To further his plan and to provide finance, Livingston made contact with some highly placed Whigs in William's parliament, where the scheme appealed to their greed. The Whigs, led by the future and cash strapped New England Governor Lord Bellomont, gave him secret orders signed by King William and commissioned a new fighting vessel, the *Adventure* galley, which was made in Deptford in just five weeks. The ship was built to Kidd's own specification, 287 tons and 36 guns and unusually, for the time, equipped with oars or sweeps for close action.

It was then up to Kidd to provision and crew her, and to do this he sold the *Antigua* to raise funds for the campaign which was to be in the Indian Ocean, exactly where Henry Avery had achieved notoriety. His problems were exacerbated by yet another threat of invasion from France, but when Admiral Shovell blasted the French fleet in Calais, he had the all clear to set sail. While sailing into the English Channel however, Kidd was in trouble with the Royal Navy for failing to acknowledge their authority. He thought his commission would prevent his men from being pressed but he promptly lost 35 men for his lack of respect. He complained to his backers and got 35 crew back – but not the same men; the replacements were mostly trouble makers nobody else wanted.

Instead of Madagascar he sailed home to New York to finally equip for the mission, picking up more dubious crew members, some of whom were responsible for stealing his *Blessed William*. He finally started his voyage in late 1696 and by the time they rounded the Cape of Good Hope and into the Indian Ocean the crew were already restless at not having seen a prize. He clashed again with authority, this time in the guise of an East India Company merchant, who disliked Kidd's manner, telling all and sundry that he was no more than a pirate, adding to the reputation he had already garnered with the Royal Navy. After a lengthy voyage, with scurvy and disease breaking out plus a leaking ship, the would-be privateers landed at Madagascar, already a known pirate haunt, to re-supply and careen their vessel. The island was illegally supplied by New York merchants, some of whom were of William's acquaintance. With no pirates or French ships in view he then headed north to the Red Sea to try his luck there. It was here his motives were questioned, was he really after pirates or a rich treasure laden Moslem ship?

In answer Kidd tried to engage one of the Arab fleets but was beaten off by an East India Company ship and then with no other prey around he sailed away, only to encounter two Portuguese war ships, where once again he gave a good account of himself when fighting them off. The *Adventure* was repaired and they then took a couple of small Arabian prizes, but all the while the crew were growing restless at the lack of real reward. This resulted in arguments which led to the death of one of the gunners who had the temerity to question the lack of success. The gunner's name was Moore and he had been exchanged for one of Kidd's pressed seamen; allegedly Kidd had called him a 'lousy dog' and in a rage threw an iron bound bucket at the man. It struck him above the right ear and Moore died the next day of a fractured skull. This 'crime' would eventually lead to Kidd's execution and through-out the voyage his fellow seamen accused him of a being *a lusty fellow,* always ready with his fists or to draw his pistols. It's hard to imagine how anyone can exert control over a gang of greedy cut-throats though, and Kidd had his own management style.

By January 1698 and late for their return home, they spied the prize they had been seeking and attacked one of the great Mogul's fleet, replete with an English captain and safe conduct pass from the French - she was a massive Armenian ship of over 400 tons, laden with silks, rubies, emeralds, gold nuggets, opium and other treasures. She was called the *Quedah Merchant.* Kidd and his crew had hit the jackpot, with the possibility of making themselves fabulously wealthy and doubling their backer's money; they just had to get their prize home. They set sail for Madagascar and promptly encountered a pirate ship the *Mocha Frigate,* captained by no less a personage than Robert Culliford, his former shipmate and

mutineer, both heading for the same pirate haven of St Mary's. Here Kidd encountered a major problem, his men refused to fight. Worse than that, all bar thirteen men went over to the pirates' cause.

To this day, treasure hunters are searching the Indian Ocean for Kidd's buried plunder.

Loot from the Quedah was divvied up and Kidd was given a privateer's share of 40%, which he was not happy about. He barricaded himself into his captain's cabin and remained confined for weeks repelling threats of murder until he finally gave in and swore an oath of allegiance to Culliford. The pirates sailed away leaving the *Adventure* galley stranded on a sand bank with her vastly depleted crew rueing the loss of their fortune. Kidd had no option but to try and limp home in the *Quedah Merchant,* with a depleted fortune and wanted by the authorities who had been studying Kidd's activities with increasing rage. A warrant had been issued for his arrest and with both the

Royal Navy and East India Company on the look out for him and he decided to sneak home via the Caribbean. He made a few trades with his exotic looking ship and quietly slipped up America's coast before getting home and having a run in with the treacherous Bellomont. Despite his pleas, and a few sweeteners, the shady Governor had him clapped in irons and sent to London for trial while his sea chest was rumoured to have ended up in Bristol's Custom House.

Several questions have to be asked about Kidd's conduct on his return home to New York, why did he hide his ship in the Caribbean stuffed full of exotic silks from the East and why did he skulk around America's Eastern seaboard, burying treasure and sounding people out, before presenting himself? The trial was a long and frustrating one with vested interests to the fore. The political scene had changed in London and the Tories were now in control, keen to expose Whig duplicity, but drawing the line at getting the King embroiled. To placate Aurangzeb, the Emperor of the Great Mogul Empire and to permit the East India Company to continue trading, Kidd was hanged at Execution Dock at Wapping in May 1701.

Lord Bellomont who died of gout just before Kidd was sentenced to death, ended up penniless despite having Kidd's treasure in his grasp. He thought the largest diamond was 'Bristol Stone' (a transparent rock crystal resembling a diamond in brilliancy and found in Clifton limestone) but it fetched £25 on its own, with the rest of the treasure that was brought back to England raising £5,500, a big sum for those days. Captain Kidd's corpse was then tarred and put into a custom built cage for all to see on their arrival at Tilbury, as a salutary lesson to one and all.

In 1706, after his death, Kidd's 'friend' Livingston petitioned the House of Lords for his share of the money from the voyage, but Parliament had already decided that it would go to the making of the new Hospital at Greenwich, another Wren masterpiece, the sailors' equivalent of the soldiers' refuge at Chelsea.

Kidd's grisly end at Execution Dock.

The Pirate Pinnacle – 'The Golden Age'

Ironically, when George I, disparagingly called the 'Turnip Man' by the pirates, ascended to the British throne it inadvertently heralded the pinnacle of the Pirates Golden Age. Woodes Rogers' arrival on New Providence in 1718 as a pirate hunter started a wave of piracy away from their Caribbean bases that led to a halt in world commerce - until the pirate genie could be put back into its bottle.

Drawing on the work of Captain Johnson, Robert Louis Stevenson used this period extensively as an underlying theme to *Treasure Island*. In one of the pivotal episodes, Long John Silver is discussing mutiny with his fellow pirates while young Jim Hawkins is memorably listening in the famous apple barrel….

"But," asked Dick, "When do we lay 'em athwart, what are we to do with 'em, anyhew?" "That's the man for me!" cried Silver admiringly. "That's what I call business, well, what would you think? Put 'em ashore like maroons? That would have been England's way. Or cut 'em down like that much pork? That would have been Flints or Billy Bones'." "Billy was the man for that," said Israel, "'Dead men don't bite' says he, well he's dead now hisself." "Right you are" said Silver, "Rough and ready. But this time it's serious. Dooty is dooty, mates. I give my vote – death." "John," cries the coxswain Hands, "You're a man!" "You'll say so, Israel, when you see," said Silver, "only one thing I claim – I claim Trelawney. I'll wring his calf's head off his body with these hands."

As we shall see, many of these characters emulated real people, but today people remember Israel Hands and Ben Gunn for their fictional roles, rather than for their contribution to piracy or Britain's early 18th Century overseas trade. Stevenson clearly enjoyed the excitement of these times and picked on various actual events and incidents to use in his fiction.

The major European powers of the day hardly ever spoke with one voice, and with their perpetual distrust of one another the pirates thrived, culminating in a pirate force that could have revolutionised the world – had it not been so unwieldy. The following vignettes show how a variety of assorted and unlikely looking characters took over the mantle of leadership that led to this epic battle between the forces of state and individualism.

Capt. Blackbeard's flag.

Blackbeard's early life is shrouded in mystery. Academics argue over his birth place and his birth date. Some say 1680, and even his original name, which has at least three variations; Edward.Teach, Edward Thatch or even Edward Drummond. In Bristol his memory is a mixture of both denial and proud son. Local legend persists that he was born in Redcliffe.

What is known isn't very savoury. He was thought to have had 14 wives, but how many were 'port wives' isn't clear. He served with Benjamin Hornigold and was given command of one of his prizes, a French Guineaman or slave ship named *La Concorde*, which he renamed *Queen Anne's Revenge* (some pirates had Jacobite sympathies) and he made the Bahamas his home during its 'Pirate Republic' heyday, two years prior to Woodes Rogers' arrival.

Why pirates had Jacobite sympathies at all is a bit of a mystery, especially in the West Country, where many suffered brutal suppression from King James II and his henchmen after the Monmouth Rebellion. It has been suggested that it was a way of legitimising pirate activities against the Crown after the Glorious Revolution of 1688, but back to Blackbeard.

Blackbeard in his prime.

At the edge of the township in the Bahamas, Blackbeard held his court under a wild fig tree. Johnson says: ….

He used to sit in council amongst his banditti, concerting or promulgating and exercising the authority of a magistrate. It is said that under the tree he kept a barrel of rum from which all who passed by were invited to drink. Those who hesitated were given a choice of drinking or being shot.

Coincidentally several wild fig trees grow today in Bristol, one of which is opposite the old Georges Brewery in Castle Park, actually growing out of the river wall.

Captain Johnson had fun describing Blackbeard, and the following description again originates in his *General History* of 1724. However, decency prevents me from using the anecdote regarding the pirate's last wife, a fifteen year old plantation owner's daughter….

Teach, the most colourful and well-known of all the pirates is a never dying legend. He was a massive man noted for his boldness, fiendish appearance and roguish ways. With cutlasses and three brace of pistols slung about him, he resembled a walking arsenal. His long black beard was twisted with brightly coloured ribbons and turned about his ears. Slow burning fuses (or matches) tucked under his hat wreathed his head with demonic smoke. All this, together with his fierce and wild eyes made him such a figure that imagination cannot form an idea of a fury from hell to look more frightful.

One day at sea he said to a few of his men…. "come, let us make a hell of our own, and try how long we can bear it". He took them below, closed up the hatches and set on fire several pots filled with brimstone and other acrid matter. One by one, close to suffocation, the men were forced to seek the upper deck. Blackbeard held out the longest and was quite pleased that he was better fitted to live in hell than the others.

Israel Hands' first mention comes soon after this episode when Teach's crew capture a sloop named the *Adventure* under David Harriot, master…. *The pirates took him and his men aboard the great ship, and sent a number of other hands with Israel Hands, master of Teach's ship, to man the sloop for the piratical account.*

His next mention is after Blackbeard takes to terrorizing the people of Carolina, where he lay off the bar of Charles Town, seizing control of all ship movements and bullying the inhabitants with his brother rogues until they paid 'Tribute'. Johnson states that….

From the bar of Charles Town they sailed to North Carolina, Captain Teach in the ship which they called the man-of-war, Captain Richards and Captain Hands in the sloops, which they now termed privateers, and another sloop serving them as tender, Teach began now to think of breaking up the company, and securing the money and the best of the effects for himself and some others of his companions he had most friendship for, and to cheat the rest. Accordingly, on pretence of running into Topsail Inlet to clean, he grounded the ship, and then, as if it had been done undesignedly and by accident, he ordered Hands' sloop to come to his assistance and get him off again, which he endeavouring to do, ran the sloop on shore near the other, and so were both lost. This done, Teach goes into the tender sloop, with forty hands and leaves the Revenge there; then takes seventeen others and maroons them upon a small sandy island about a league from the main, where there is neither bird, beast or herb for their subsistence, and where they would have perished if Major Bonnet had not two days after taken them off.

Stede-Bonnet was mocked by Blackbeard and his gang for his poor seamanship and was unluckily captured by Captain Rhett when seeking Charles Vane. He had a reputation for callous and brutal behaviour, especially towards women, but when he went to the gallows he was dragged sobbing and pleading for mercy. Bonnet was hung in November 1718.

Another version of the marooning story is that in the early 1700s Blackbeard is said to have punished a mutinous crew by marooning them on Dead Man's Chest, a small remote island in the British Virgin Islands chain, without water or landing places. Seventy five men were given a cutlass and a bottle of rum and Teach's hope was that they would all kill each other off, but when he returned at the end of 30 days he was surprised to find that 15 had survived.

Stevenson used the following verse throughout *Treasure Island,* but whichever story you choose to believe, they both led to the same deadly and macabre outcome….

Fifteen men on the dead man's chest,
Yo ho ho ho, and a bottle of rum!
Drink and the devil had done for the rest,
Yo ho ho ho, and a bottle of rum!

Teach went off to North Carolina where he settled down for a while and lived the life of a local celebrity; he married a plantation owner's daughter and was the toast of the local planters, even courting the Governor, Charles Eden, Esq. He surrendered to His Majesty's proclamation, but he couldn't resist falling back into his old ways and even though Eden ran with the foxes as well as the hounds, not all of the Governors in the area were as lenient. Step forward Lieutenant Governor Spottiswood, who published 'A Proclamation'…. *for apprehending or killing pyrates.* Spottiswood, a friend and colleague of Woodes Rogers, brought in the Royal Navy to finish Blackbeard off.

Immediately prior to this, Israel Hands and Blackbeard's pilot, Marshall, were drinking together, and without provocation Teach drew out a pair of pistols and cocked them under the table. When he was ready, he crossed them and fired. Hands was shot through the knee and so missed the last engagement. When asked why he had done this, Teach said, "Damn you all! Unless I now and then kill one of my men, they will forget who I am".

The man sent by the Royal Navy to terminate Blackbeard's career was Lieutenant Robert Maynard in his sloop the *Pearl*. On 22nd November 1718 Maynard tricked him into battle off Ocracoke. After a savage encounter, in which Blackbeard sustained over 20 cuts and at least 5 shots, he was killed and decapitated. Legend has it that his headless body was thrown overboard and swam round his ship 3 times before disappearing. Of Maynard's men, 10 were killed and 24 were wounded.

As was the custom with a pirate, his head was hung from the bowsprit, and the skull ended up as a drinking vessel in a tavern in Williamsburg. The authorities caught up with Hands and would have hanged him as well had he not been reprieved at the last minute by a proclamation prolonging the pirates' pardon. Johnson states that he finished his days in London a poor lame beggar and seems to have missed the huge similarity between Israel Hands' name and that of one of Black Bart Roberts's crew, Israel Hynde, who met a grisly end in 1722.

According to Captain Johnson, here are the names of the pirates killed in the engagement:-

Edward Teach, Commander
Philip Morton, gunner
Garret Gibbens, boatswain
Owen Roberts, carpenter
Thomas Miller, quartermaster
John Husk
Joseph Curtice
Joseph Brookes (1)
Nathaniel Jackson

All the rest, except the two last, were wounded and afterwards hanged in Virginia.

John Carnes
Joseph Brooks (2)
James Blake
John Gills
Thomas Gates
James White
Richard Stiles
Caesar
Joseph Philips
James Robbins
John Martin
Edward Salter
Stephen Daniel
Richard Greensail
Samuel Odel, acquitted
Israel Hands, pardoned

The prize for Maynard's brave men who risked life and limb was £2,500 divided equally amongst the companies of his two ships, the *Lime* and the *Pearl*. The money was the proceeds of Blackbeard's 'Treasure' – 25 hogsheads of sugar, 11 tierces, 145 bags of cocoa, a barrel of indigo, and a bale of cotton, along with the sale of Blackbeard's sloop and monies from the Governor and his Secretary (pursuant to their proclamation). There have been calls for a statue of Blackbeard in his home town, but some have joked that a cycle path named in his honour might be more appropriate.

The torture of Captain Skinner.

Captain Skinner was a pirate victim and the following episode comes again from Captain Johnson's *General History of ye Pyrates,* under the chapter *'The life of Captain England'....*

England was one of these men, who seemed to have a great deal of good nature, and did not want for courage; he was not avaricious and always averse to the ill usage prisoners received. He would have been contented with moderate plunder, and less mischievous pranks, could his companions have been brought to the same temper, but he was generally overruled, and as he was engaged in that abominable society, he obliged to be a partner in all their vile actions.

Captain England sailed to the coast of Africa, after the island of Providence was settled by the English government [Woodes Rogers], and the pirates surrendered to His Majesty's proclamation, and took several ships and vessels, particularly the Cadogan snow belonging to Bristol at Sierra Leone, one Skinner master, who was inhumanly murdered by some of his crew, that had lately been his own men, and served in said vessel. It seems some quarrel had happened between them, so that Skinner thought fit to remove these fellows on board of a man-of-war, and at the same time refused them their wages. Not long after they found means to desert that service, and shipping themselves aboard a sloop in the West Indies, was taken by a pirate, and brought to Providence, and sailed along the same account along with Captain England.

As soon as Skinner had struck to the pirate, he was ordered to come on board in his boat, which he did, and the person that he first cast his eye upon, proved to be his old boatswain, who stared him in the face like his evil genius, and accosted him in this manner. 'Ah, Captain Skinner! Is it you? The only man I wish to see; I am much in your debt, and now I shall pay you all in your own coin.'

The poor man trembled every joint, when he found into what company he had fallen, and dreaded the event, as he had reason enough to do; for the boatswain immediately called to his consorts, laid hold of the captain, and made him fast to the windless, and there pelted him with glass bottles, which cut him in a sad manner; after which they whipped him about the deck, till they were weary, being deaf to all his prayers and entreaties, and at last, because he had been a good master to his men, they said he should have an easy death, and so shot him through the head. They took some few things out the snow, but gave the vessel and all her cargo to Howel Davis the mate, and the rest of the crew, as will be hereafter mentioned in the chapter of Captain Davis.

Captain England's flag.

Edward England was very well regarded but didn't seem to have the steely edge required to control a band of cut-throats. This was not uncommon, many pirate captains were appointed for virtues other than that of controlling their men, that fell to the quartermaster and the best ones ruled with a rod of iron. What the men wanted from their captain was primarily good fortune, good sense and good seamanship. Captain England was Irish and whilst innocently sailing between Jamaica and Providence in 1717, was taken by pirate Captain Winter. As was common he decided to join the pirate band and ended captaining his own pirate ship the *Pearl* to West Africa, just prior to Rogers' arrival in New Providence. Poorly defended, the Guinea coast was ripe for the picking and within no time England and his crew had more than ten prizes under their belt.

One of them was the Bristol slave ship the *Peterborough* which the pirates found suitable for their own means, renaming it the *Victory*. With the disgruntled and cruel ex-Royal Navy man John Taylor acting as captain, the *Victory* and the *Fancy* then sailed in consort. Success brought more and more followers and by the time the crews had voted to do the 'pirate round', they had swollen to over 200 men, many of whom having already shown their credentials with gross acts of barbarity.

It was while cruising for rich victims in the Indian Ocean that England's career became undone. They came across a fat British East Indiaman named the *Cassandra*, captained by a John Mackry (Macrae) who put up a stiff fight, which was against the pirate code; no mercy should be given to any ship showing resistance. England prevented his blood thirsty crew from killing Macrae and even managed to get him put safely ashore with some of his cargo in the badly damaged *Fancy*, but the arguments that ensued led to his fellow pirate captain, John Taylor, taking over command.

Worse was to follow, England and three others who had also argued for leniency, were marooned on the island of Mauritius. This was contrary to what Long John Silver said about him…. *"That's what I call business. Well, what would you think? Put'em ashore like maroons? That would have been England's way."* In reality England and his mates, including a bearded sailor with one leg (another prototype for Silver?) escaped their island prison by making a raft and drifting for over 500 miles to

A forerunner of Long John Silver?

Madagascar. England died in poverty there by the end of 1720.

Taylor took control of the Cassandra and put French pirate La Buze in command of the *Victory* where they went on to capture a huge and fabulously wealthy Portuguese East Indiaman *Virgem de Cabo* that happened to be recovering from storm damage on the island of Bourbon, nowadays called Reunion. On board was the Count of Ericeria, about the only one to put up a stout resistance and for that he was spared, but the personal fortune that he amassed in Goa was lost along with a huge consignment of diamonds bound for his king.

Taylor's gang had hit the jackpot, and their haul was said to be the biggest ever taken in the Golden Age. After trying to procure more prizes, they realised they were the 'worlds most wanted' and after they divided up the booty they went their separate ways. Taylor ended up in Cuba after taking a commission in a Spanish man-of-war attacking English logwood cutters in the bay of Honduras. This cruel man was never brought to justice.

Howell Davis was presented with Skinner's former ship the *Cadogan,* after Skinner's fatal encounter with England's men, sailing her with the remaining crew to Barbados. The authorities didn't believe Davis' story and clapped him in jail for three months until he could convince

them of his innocence, but with his name blackened by the events surrounding Skinner's death he found it hard to get gainful employment.

Fetching up in New Providence at about the same time as Woodes Rogers he took some time to get a berth on Rogers' intended supply ship the *Buck,* where he managed to get passage as an ordinary seaman. Rogers' position was getting dire as he was running out of supplies; he resorted to sending off two ships to illegally trade with the Spanish to bolster his reserves, but this proved unwise. The *Buck's* crew consisted mainly of pardoned pirates and when the opportunity arose they seized the ship.

Walter Kennedy, Dennis Topping, Thomas Anstis, Christopher Moody and William Magness all accompanied Davis in his venture and *over a large bowl of punch* they elected the short stocky Welshman from Milford Haven captain. Their next act was to draw up articles and make *a declaration of war against the whole world.* After careening in Cuba, fighting off the French and taking a few prizes in the rich shipping lanes off Hispaniola, they decided to cross the Atlantic and try their luck elsewhere, ending up at the Cape Verde Islands.

By now the crew had grown to over 60 men, on a ship usually accustomed to only 15, with the aforementioned pirates making up the 'House of Lords' and including such pirate luminaries as quartermaster John Taylor (whom we have met before) and wild gunner Henry Dennis. Using subterfuge, Davis managed to trick his way into the Portuguese Governor of St Nicholas's good books and for over a month his men were able to trade their goods for favours from the locals.

After their bout of rest and relaxation, Davis' crew were ready for more action and within weeks they took prize after prize in the shipping lanes off the Isle of May (Mayo), one of which had 26 guns which they took for their own use, renaming her *King James.* The Portuguese Governor of Mayo foolishly told Davis that he suspected him and his men of being pirates; this so greatly affronted them that they promptly took the fortress and sacked it.

With each prize, more and more seamen came over to Davis' cause, encouraging him to expand his operations; he tricked the Governor of Gambia Castle into thinking they were traders from Liverpool in search of gum and elephants teeth, and when granted an audience Davis promptly put a pistol to the Governor's breast. The Castle and all of its riches gained from the slave trade were given up without a fight. Davis' crew torched the Castle after ransacking it and then caroused for two days until a menacing sail hove into view. Davis prepared his men to fight before realising it was a fellow pirate ship, captained by Oliver le Vasseur, better known as la Bouche or la Buze – the Buzzard; with a joint crew of about 64 equally split between Africans and Frenchmen. After an exchange of salutes they both raised their black flags and the two joined up sailing for Sierra Leone together.

Here they encountered yet another pirate captain, Thomas Cocklyn, a cruel and savage man not universally liked – he'd already crossed swords with one of the 'House of Lords', Christopher Moody; but for the sake of confederacy the brethren decided to team up to attack the local fort which put up some resistance until the full strength of the pirate force became apparent. They stayed at the fort for nearly two months, taking another vessel for La Buze before careening their remaining ships, taking stock and sailing off in consort together. Davis had trouble with his quartermaster John Taylor who managed to depose him as captain, but when his vicious vindictiveness was taken out on the crew, Taylor's reign became short-lived and

Davis was re-elected captain.

Davis was then elected commodore of this enlarged fleet but was wary of his new force and called a council of war within a short time. He told his fellow pirate captains that he had helped build up their ships but didn't trust them not to use them against him. They immediately parted with each going their separate ways. Cocklyn, who had welcomed Taylor to his ship, was later caught and hanged while the Buzzard ultimately teamed up with England, as we have seen.

Free from his confederates, Walter Kennedy took over Taylor's role as quartermaster and Davis sailed back down the coast of Africa looking for yet more prizes when he came across the *Marquis del Campo,* a Dutch merchantman of 30 guns, who immediately fired a broadside into the *King James.* Davis was in a mood for fighting, and fight he did, with the battle lasting nearly a day until he was victorious; Davis renamed his new acquisition the *Royal Rover.*

Davis' fleet was getting more and more formidable, and his next target was three British slave ships at Anamabu. With their captains ashore buying slaves they were given up without a fight. The ships were already partially loaded with slaves and a considerable weight of gold dust which soon became the pirate's property. One of the ships, the *Princess of London,* had a certain second mate who would ultimately take Davis' mantle and become the most successful pirate ever, 'Black' Bart Roberts.

Just after leaving Anamabu one of the lookouts spied a sail and Davis' fleet immediately made haste to chase, soon discovering her to be an even larger Dutch merchantman than the *Royal Rover* had been. After just one broadside from the pirates the Dutch gave quarter; the pirates couldn't believe what they had stumbled upon –

the Governor of Accra on board with all of his wealth. It was reported in the *Weekly Journal* of 9th April 1720 that *….The pyrates off the coast of Guinea in Africa have taken goods to the value of £204,000.*

Davis took a shine to 30 year old Roberts and befriended him after he had impressed his new captain with his vast knowledge of the triangular trade routes. To prove his knowledge Davis' squadron set a course for the Portuguese island of Principe, 600 miles south west of Anamabu. Here he tried his familiar ruse of pretending to be something he wasn't, this time a British man-of-war. Flying the navy's colours he flagged for the Governor to have a 'parley', but this time he'd met his match.

The Governor had apparently heard of the trickery meted out on the Gambia Castle and turned tables on the wily Welshman by fooling him into an unsafe rendezvous. He had agreed to a meeting on the *Royal Rover* but had invited Davis to his fort for a drink before rowing out to the ship. On this fools errand Davis and his party were ambushed by a group of musketeers, all but two being killed. Davis was shot through the bowels but managed to discharge his pistols *….thus like a gamecock, giving a dying blow that he might not fall unrevenged.* Walter

Pirate diplomacy.

Kennedy was one of the survivors and advised Davis' remaining crew of the treachery.

Stevenson also immortalised Davis, in another episode from his apple barrel scene he set down the following dialogue .... *Ah! cried another voice, that of the youngest hand on board, and evidently full of admiration, 'he was the flower of the flock, was Flint!' 'Davis was a man, too, by all accounts,' said Silver.*

'The House of Lords'* needed a new leader and Davis' protégé, Roberts, was given the role, whereupon he immediately agreed to avenge the death of the well liked Davis. Roberts sent Kennedy and 30 of the men overland against the fort which they razed to the ground and then under cover of their ships guns, set fire to the township, including two Portuguese ships in the harbour. The pirates took another two prizes before sailing off.

Captain Jack Rackham's flag.

'Calico Jack' and his wicked wenches came to the fore in late October 1720 when reports reached the Governor of Jamaica that a band of pirates were wreaking havoc along the coast. On hearing the news he immediately released a heavily manned Sloop, captained by Jonathan Barnet, *a brisk fellow*, to bring them in. With a favourable wind and

* *Pirate council.*

little resistance, Barnet captured one of the most notorious of the Caribbean pirate bands, that of Captain Jack Rackam (or Rackham).

Rackam first rose to notoriety when Woodes Rogers arrived at New Providence to issue the Kings Pardon in 1718. One crew, captained by Charles Vane, was having none of it and broke away from the feared ex-privateer; Rackam was Vane's quartermaster and about six months after their escape he eventually tired of Vane's cruel ways, taking his brigantine from him after he refused to attack a French man-of-war. He then set up on his own account.

He got the nickname of 'Calico' because of his penchant for wearing cotton in the sultry Caribbean where, according to Captain Johnson, he enjoyed a life suited to his crew's *depraved tempers*. After achieving a modicum of success he changed his mind and decided to finally take the King's Pardon from Woodes Rogers. This was in May 1719, and it was in a tavern in Nassau that he fell in love with another's wife – Anne Bonny, wife of small time pirate James Bonny, informer to Woodes Rogers himself.

Bonny managed to get his wife tried for adultery with Rackam and Rogers found her guilty, ordering her to be flogged and returned to her husband; but before this could happen Anne and Calico Jack eloped, seizing the *Curlew* with some of Jack's old shipmates. Being one of the fastest sloops around, the pair soon made good their escape with Anne dressed as man – women on board were regarded as bad luck. They eventually had a child together and left the baby in Cuba with some pirate families. When the pair's money ran out, Rackam went back to his old ways, and began terrorising the Caribbean once again.

In league with Anne, Calico Jack and his henchmen captured many prizes, including a Dutch ship. After plundering the vessel they took prisoners and to his great surprise, Rackam found Anne cuddled up to one of them, who appeared to be a Dutch boy. His jealous rage eased a bit when he realised that Anne's companion was of her own sex, turning out to be none other than Mary Read, destined to join pirate folklore along with Anne. Both women had fascinating lives before they went 'on the account' overcoming many of life's obstacles in their own inimitable way.

Anne was the illegitimate daughter of William Cormac, an eminent Cork lawyer who became a successful plantation owner in South Carolina after leaving Ireland to live in peace with Anne's mother. By the age of 12 Anne was rich and something of a beauty with several suitors, but on the negative side she was headstrong and temperamen-

tal. On one occasion she stabbed a servant girl with a knife and on another she beat up a young lad for trying to rape her, although you can't blame her for that. She finally fell for a ne'er-do well, James Bonny, but after being denied her fortune by her father, they ran away to New Providence together for Anne to meet her date with destiny.

Mary Read was born in London, also out of wedlock, and spent most of her childhood dressed as a boy, running away to sea as soon as she was able. She ended up in Flanders, incredibly serving in the Dutch army amongst Marlborough's allies during the Spanish war. Here she met and fell in love with one of her fellow troopers and at the end of one of the campaigns she shed her uniform and married him. Their love was not to last however, her hus-

Anne Bonny and Mary Read shown here as a right pair of bruisers.

band dying of fever. This left Mary to run the inn they owned without help. This didn't suit Mary and she decided to go to sea again, only to be taken by Rackam and his crew.

The women carried on their subterfuge by wearing men's clothing and eyewitness accounts stated that they were more accomplished fighters than the men. During their trial, after capture by Barnet, it was said of them that, "In times of action, no persons among them were more resolute, or ready to board, or undertake anything that was hazardous, than Anne or Mary". To avoid the noose they were found to be 'quick with child' and Anne had the satisfaction of saying some final comforting words to 'Calico Jack' before he met his maker…. "If you had fought like a man you wouldn't have to hang like a dog. Do straighten yourself up!" Mary apparently died of fever during childbirth in gaol, but it was rumoured Anne got away and became the mistress of a former Red Sea privateer in Charlestown.

As a footnote, anecdotal evidence suggests that both John Rackam and James Bonny were Bristolians. In all, over a dozen pirates were hung and controversially some were only drinking companions that they had met by chance, but one of the genuine crew members, Carty (or Macarty) also went to his death with a famous quote…. "My friends said I would die with my shoes on. To make'em liars, I kicks them off!" He was defiant to the end. The trial of Jack and his shipmates marked the beginning of the end of the 'Golden Age of Piracy'.

Captain Robert's flag.

Black Bart Roberts was born in Pembrokeshire in 1682, and his real name was John Roberts; he'd seen action with the navy in the Spanish war but was reduced to serving on slave ships with little chance of a captaincy until his chance encounter with Davis. After his appointment by the 'House of Lords', he inherited all of Davis' fighting force including the *Royal Rover* and her consort the *Fortune* and he decided to leave Africa for a while and try his luck off Brazil.

After an immaculate crossing of the Atlantic the cruise was proving unprofitable until they headed north and came across a newly assembled Portuguese treasure fleet of 32 ships packed with gold, silver, tobacco, sugar and skins. After a quick assessment of the enemy force the pirates decided on one of the boldest moves in pirate history; they sailed into the heart of the fleet and plucked out the largest plum – the *Sagrada Familia* complete with 36 guns.

In an amazing feat of bluff and bravery, Roberts' men, under quartermaster Walter Kennedy, boarded the huge target and with the loss of just two men captured the prize and used the *Royal Rover* to tow her out of the bay. Just one of the Portuguese men-of-war offered resistance but a swift broadside put a halt to any gallantry The action was later reported in the *Weekly Journal* where the *Royal Rover* was contemptuously described as *formerly an English hog-boat.** Hog-boat or not, the haul was massive and even included some of the King's treasure, not least a diamond encrusted gold cross which Roberts took to wearing himself when going into battle.

* *Supply vessel*

The pirates escaped pursuit by heading for Devil's Island, then a Spanish possession but latterly made famous by the French as a notorious penal colony, where they were able to take stock once again against the backdrop of fiddle playing and trumpets. The 'Lords' then decided to carry on northward to the West Indies but prior to gathering their force together they went after prizes once again; with the *Royal Ranger* being careened Roberts took the *Fortune* to hunt them down. This ended in disaster when a big prize eluded him and he became becalmed, severely running out of supplies.

Roberts sent for the *Royal Ranger* only to be told that Walter Kennedy had deserted him taking the ship, all of its crew and the treasure ship with him. Roberts and the 'House of Lords' were beside themselves with rage and forthwith banned all Irishmen from joining them; to prevent any repetition of this and to control the men, all of the crew had to sign up to new Articles compiled by Roberts. These included the right to vote on affairs, to keep their Piece (weapon) clean and *No Boy or Woman to be allowed amongst them* – punishment death.

Kennedy ultimately made it back to Deptford where he kept a 'bawdy house' and dipping back into his former profession when it suited; this worked well until one of his whores turned evidence against him and after a bit of trickery by the powers that be he was found out, sentenced to death and hung at Execution Dock in the middle of 1721.

Black Bart carried on cruising though, desperately trying to

restore his fortune; his crew took several small prizes but no ship large enough to transfer to. He teamed up with another pirate called La Palisse to strengthen his hand, but with pirates like 'Calico Jack' active in the area, targets were getting scarce and the authorities were finally beginning to take notice. Two Royal Navy ships on patrol were redirected and Governor Lowther of Barbados commissioned two privateers to try and stop the pirates; the latter course of action nearly worked.

Captains Rogers and Greaves were given command of the 16 gun *Summersett* and 10 gun *Philippa* respectively and their mission was to specifically attack Black Bart's 12 gun sloop *Fortune*. In February 1720 the combatant ships made sight of one another and to Roberts' good luck he had La Pelisse in the *Sea King* as consort; this put the dampeners on Greaves' will to fight. Pretending to be merchantmen, *Summersett* and *Philippa* seemed easy targets for the pirates but on closer inspection La Pelisse got cold feet, firing a broadside and then fleeing the engagement.

Roberts and the *Fortune* were made of sterner stuff however and the remaining pirates attacked, guns blazing and band playing. They even towed their bow chaser crammed with men armed to the teeth and ready to board at any moment. Broadsides were exchanged but the *Philippa* proved to be a millstone around Rogers' neck, often getting in the way and failing to fire in support of the action.

By the time the *Summersett*

had the upper hand, with the *Fortune* badly holed below the water line, Rogers wanted just one more broadside to finish her off but was prevented from doing so by the feckless Greaves who mutely sailed into the firing line. Roberts saw his opportunity and disengaged the action and fled, putting on all sails and continuing to use the *Philippa* as a shield.

Many men on both sides were killed or injured in the action, with Roberts losing almost half of his 70 man crew before finding a safe haven in Dominica to recuperate. As Owen Rogers and the *Summersett* galley were both from Bristol, all things Bristol were added to Irishmen and Barbadians on Roberts' hate list. The list soon expanded to include Martinique as the French Governor there did his best to try and capture Roberts and his men while they were at their weakest.

Two French sloops had been despatched to pursue Roberts, narrowly missing him every time until the pirates had managed to make repairs, re-supply and head north again, this time to the Newfoundland fishing banks. Prior to their departure, Roberts had convened a meeting of the 'House of Lords' to discuss his new plan of action. This was to attack ships while they were at anchor, preventing a repetition of the surprise they received from Rogers and setting up an opportunity to attack the ports that supplied the ships. All agreed. Roberts then vowed to have the Governors of Barbados and Martinique one day swinging from his yard arm. To celebrate he had some new flags made, one depicting himself astride two skulls with the letters ABH and AMH on them – a Barbadian's head and a Martinican's head.

From July to September Black Bart took prizes at will, even entering harbours and terrifying massive fleets at anchor; nothing could stop him. On one of these forays into the port of Trepassey he managed to secure a succes-sor to the *Fortune* called the *Bristol,* a 16 gun brig under a Captain Copplestone; Roberts renamed her *Good Fortune.* A massive 150 fishing vessels and dozens of merchantmen succumbed to the pirates as their ranks swelled with volunteers from the prizes. Transatlantic shipping almost ceased and the American colonies began to wonder if they wouldn't be better off as an independent nation where their taxes could afford better protection than they were getting from the British Government. Captain Roberts quietly slipped southward to the Caribbean once again. Once there Roberts and his men used the opportunity to 'fence' some of their ill gotten gains and careen their ships. La Palisse in the *Sea King* had joined up once more and together with Black Bart's crew engaged in the pirate version of 'rest and recreation'.

It didn't take the pirates long to get back to their pillaging best and the area soon became a hunting ground of the worst kind. No ship or person was safe and if resistance was presented no mercy was shown. A Scottish sailor named Richard Luntley, who had been taken by Davis, was accused of mutinous talk and marooned by Roberts for his troubles only to be rescued by a merchantman who got him home to stand trial for consorting with the 'great Pyrate'. He was hanged at Leith.

A large Dutch interloper was only taken after a bloody fight in the harbour of St Lucia; the 30 gun ship couldn't manoeuvre and was at the mercy of Roberts's full fleet that had raced in, band blaring and guns firing. The Dutch gave no quarter and after a four hour fight there were many dead on both sides. The 15 survivors of the Dutchman's crew of 90 were immediately slaughtered and every person of Dutch descent that the pirates could reach was also killed in an orgy of violence. Black Bart then claimed the Dutch ship to be his next flagship and renamed her *Royal Fortune.*

Roberts now sensed that the authorities would once again be on his case and decided to leave the West Indies, this time to venture back to Africa, but nature was against him this time and his fleet were blown back to the Americas, desperately short of water. They landed at Surinam to re-provision and then headed north once more to wreak revenge on two of Roberts' avowed enemies, the Governors of Martinique and Barbados.

Taking prizes was easy for Roberts and his cronies. As they took more and more ships of every nationality the pirates' only problem seemed to be trading their goods for yet more gold. Always keeping one step ahead of the law the pirates stumbled across a large French man-of-war which should have resisted them. Roberts couldn't believe his luck when the ship's most important passenger turned out to be none other than the Governor of Martinique. who was promptly hanged from the yard arm, fulfilling one of Black Bart's promises.

By April 1721, Robert's fleet was now three strong, the *Royal Fortune,* the *Good Fortune* and the *Sea King,* all fully laden with booty. Prizes were getting scarce, sensible merchantmen avoiding the area. All the while the threat of capture was getting greater so the pirates' decided to try again for Africa. They were unaware that their barbarous actions were beginning to make people tire of their activities and the Piracy Act of 1721 came into being; these extended the penalties for piracy to anyone who *shall trade with, truck, barter or exchange* with them. They were also unaware of *HMS' Swallow* and *Weymouth* travelling to the Guinea Coast to protect British interests in the slave trade.

On the crossing, Black Bart in the *Royal Fortune* lost contact with Thomas Anstis in the *Good Fortune,* who had decided to bid a 'soft farewell'. By this time *Anstis* and his fellow crew had had enough of the *Great Pyrate's* ways. This didn't stop Roberts however, as he and his merry band continued to rove, picking up yet more and more prizes. Anstis also carried on a-roving, ending up skewered to his hammock in 1723.

Roberts had a perpetual problem exchanging booty for supplies and money, but in Africa he was in luck; there were numerous white traders up and down the coast who were willing to trade with anybody and anything. These Europeans worked outside of the Royal Africa Company, much to their chagrin, aiding 'interlopers' and pirates alike. According to Captain Johnson, Bristol merchants for instance favoured the Rio Nune where they found a ready market for their large cargoes of beer, cider and strong liquors which they exchanged for slaves and teeth (Elephant ivory). One of these traders along the coast on the Rio Pungo was named Benjamin Gunn.

It was at Rio Nune that Roberts' cut-throats ended up, missing the *Weymouth* and the *Swallow* by just one month and hearing for the first time that their day of reckoning might not be too far away. They were also told that the Navy wouldn't return until Christmas, allowing, as Johnson recorded, the pirates *to indulge themselves.* This indulgence included the continued taking of prizes, one of which was the slaver *Onslow.* They refitted the *Onslow* with 40 guns and renamed her *Royal Fortune* and abandoned the original ship of this name.

They travelled on to Old Calabar where they upset the natives by fighting them and setting fire to their township, but this didn't distract the pirates from taking more and more ships, English, Dutch, it mattered not. Many of the prizes were from Bristol, one such being the *Mercy* galley which they took in October 1721. On board was one Israel Hands (or Hynde) who immediately went 'on the account' with Roberts, along with 7 of his shipmates. Also, from the *Cornwall* galley, arrogant ship's surgeon

Peter Scudamore joined the motley crew; he was the only surgeon ever to volunteer for service with the Black Captain, where he became one of his intimate friends, ultimately becoming a member of the 'House of Lords'.

The 'End Game' was fast approaching for Roberts as his control diminished. His crews were getting larger and larger and their lust for carousing was getting out of hand. With *HMS Swallow* and *HMS Weymouth* circling to pounce, matters were coming to a head. Roberts' fleet now consisted of the *Royal Fortune* and the *Ranger,* both powerful fighting vessels, packed with men.

By the middle of January 1722 Roberts knew that the only way to keep his men occupied was to carry on taking plunder. His fleet then made an audacious attack on the slaving port of Whydah; again their band blaring and guns blazing they seized all 12 ships in harbour – 5 Portuguese, 4 French and 3 English. All bar one ship agreed to pay the 'Gentlemen of Fortune' a ransom and the fate of the one that didn't ended in tragedy; with 80 slaves shackled below, the ship was torched leading to *A Cruelty unparalleled.*

Roberts also obtained a Royal Africa Company letter that revealed that he had been spotted by Captain Ogle's *Swallow,* making him prevent the release of captured crews for fear of supplying information. Apart from drunkenness, Roberts' other concern was disease which was ripping through his crew, but not as badly as the *Swallow's* sister ship the *Weymouth* which had lost so many crew, including Alexander Selkirk, that it was unfit for duty. Although Black Bart had just received a ransom for the Comte de Thoulouze, the ship was a former privateer from St Malo and proved to be such a trim craft he decided to take it anyway and renamed her *Great Ranger,* confusingly renaming the rest of his fleet *Little Ranger* and so on. Long John Silver's view on this was (after referring to the surgeon that removed his leg)….

"It was a master surgeon, him that ampytated me – Latin by the bucket, and what not; but he was hanged like a dog, and sun dried like the rest, at Corso Castle. That was Roberts' men, that was, and comed of changing names to their ships – 'Royal Fortune' and so on. Now, what a ship was christened, so let her stay, I says."

On the morning of 5th February off of Cape Lopez, Roberts spied *HMS Swallow* apparently coming towards the pirates but then veering off apparently to flee. Black Bart assumed it was a merchantman and decided to get the *Great Ranger,* under Skyrme, to give chase. Bolstered with extra men from the *Royal Fortune,* the pirates went after their prey, not knowing that the ship was the *Swallow* that had innocently taken avoidance action from a large shoal. Captain Ogle was fuming as he wanted to confront the pirates straight away, but when he realised he could pick the pirates off piecemeal he cheered up.

Skyrme seemed oblivious to the size of the *Swallow* and kept gaining on his intended victim until they were out of sight and earshot of the shore. As the ships closed Skyrme realised his mistake and Ogle's men let off a deadly broadside, smashing into the pirate ship above and below the water line. Taking away Skyrme's leg in the process. Under a hail of chain shot and musket fire the *Great Ranger* lost its topmast, making her un-manoeuvrable. They fought back with 'Lords' Ashplant and Valentine, along with Israel Hyndes leading them on. It was 4 hours before the action stopped, with 10 pirates killed and 20 seriously injured. Israel had one of his arms blown off and Skyrme asked for quarter. When sailors from the *Swallow* boarded they were met with a giant explosion after two surviving pirates had set off the powder magazine; the rest of the survivors were clapped in irons.

Captain Roberts with his ships 'Royal Fortune' and 'Ranger' taking 11 Slavers off the West coast of Africa.

Oblivious to the fate of the *Great Ranger,* Black Bart went a-roving again in the *Royal Fortune,* instantly taking a wealthy slaver called the *Neptune* with a large quantity of alcohol on board. As you would expect this led to much celebrating. The next day Ogle made his move, pretending to be a merchantman, he quietly moved towards his prey until Roberts was tipped off by one of the *Swallow's* deserters that this interloper was not what it appeared. The majority of the men were still in a drunken stupor and took some shaking into life; Ogle definitely had the advantage.

The Black Captain was dressed in his usual finery, his dark good looks set off by his lace shirt and ruffles with crimson robes, his diamond encrusted gold cross glistening around his neck and a large red feather in his hat. After making a quick assessment of the situation he decided, that with the crew unfit, their best course of action was to try and run for it, risking only one broadside from the *Swallow* at best. The plan nearly worked but the *Royal Fortune* got momentarily becalmed and had to withstand a withering broadside from the *Swallow,* instantly crippling the pirate ship. Swivel guns and musketry added to the pirate's plight and the well-dressed red man standing in the middle of the deck was an easy target. He was struck down by grapeshot that ripped his throat open; his comrades weighted his body down and threw him overboard. His merry life and a short one was over.

Black Bart's surviving pirates had to wait for over 6 weeks before standing trial at Cape Corso Castle on the Bight of Benin; although most pleaded their innocence, 91 pirates were found guilty with 54 sentenced to death of which 52 hanged. 74 were acquitted by the court led by Captain Mungo Herdman. He pronounced the following death penalty to the 54....

Ye and each of you are adjudged and sentenced......to the place of execution without the gates of this castle, and there within the flood marks to be hanged by the neck until you are **dead, dead, dead**. *And the Lord have mercy on your souls.*

Once again, according to Johnson's 1724 *General History of Ye Pyrates,* here is what befell Hands and his shipmates from the *Mercy,* on the 20th day of April 1722. In all likelihood they were on the slaver against their will in the first place. Executed....

Israel Hynde of Bristol	30
Cuthbert Goss of Topsham	21
Thomas Giles of Minehead	26

John Griffin from Blackwall, Middlesex was indentured; Christian Granger, Nicholas Brattle and James White were all acquitted.

Victorious Captain Challoner Ogle kept nearly all of Black Bart's treasure for himself and if it wasn't for Johnson's book they wouldn't have known of the 'head money'* that they were entitled to and which Ogle reluctantly paid. The rest of the loot, despite his men having legitimate claims upon it, Ogle kept, turning down repeated demands to hand it over.

*Prize money.

Ogle was fabulously wealthy and rose to the rank of Admiral in the navy; he was one of London's original 'Fat Cats'.

Historians agree that the Great Trial marked the end of the pirates Golden Age, never again would international commerce come to a stop in such a way. It didn't end piracy and it never will, but by the time of Johnson's book the British, Dutch and French had all taken major steps to protect their trade which proved to be effective.

Mark Steeds.

Captain Edward England in his pomp, fell foul of his colleagues and was marrooned.

The Bristol privateer 'Caesar' escourting a convoy and beating off a French frigate during the American War of Independence.

Part 3:   Privateers and Letter of Marque Ships out of Bristol.

Privateers, as the name suggests, waged private war at sea (See Appendix 3). The practice was licensed by the state in one of two ways: *Letters of Reprisals* which could be issued to merchants which authorised them to use forcible means to exact compensation from foreign merchants who had defaulted on a contract; and a *Letter of Marque* which was the instrument more commonly used. *Letters of Marque* gave authority to captains and crews to organise private ventures with the purpose of seizing ships (and sometimes settlements) of other nations at war with Britain. Privateers also acted as an auxiliary force to the Royal Navy, but operated chiefly for profit. Both *Letters* were allocated by the Lord High Admiral.

Other countries had their privateers, including the Barbary Coast corsairs. They were even active in the English and Bristol Channels, seizing European ships. The crews were taken captive and sold in the North African slave markets.

Up to the end of the seventeenth century London was the most active port for privateering ventures. However, by the beginning of the eighteenth century Bristol achieved parity with London and for some years even managed to fit out more privateers than the capital city.

The earliest record of Bristol privateers is a *Letter of Marque* granted to the masters and crew of the ships *James* and *Trinity* by Henry IV in 1405. The masters of the *James* and *Trinity* were named as John Wellys and Philip Taillour respectively. England was at war with the Welsh freedom fighter Owain Glyndwr (Owen Glendower) who had secured French allies. A large French army had succeeded in landing in Wales and Henry needed ships to prevent further incursions. Included in the Letter of Marque was a clause ….

either do not permit to be done any violence, hindrance or hurt to any who are in friendship with us.

This may have been a reminder to the privateers not to attack English or allied merchant ships who would have been an easy target; the *James* and *Trinity* would have had a substantial number of bowmen and men-at-arms on board. It seems that even as far back as 1405 there was a thin dividing line between privateer and pirate.

Conflict between the European maritime powers increased with the colonization of the Caribbean and the Americas by the Spanish. English ships were attacked whenever they tried to trade in the Spanish 'sphere of influence'. It was in effect an undeclared state of war. However, in 1585 a formal declaration of war was announced which lasted until 1604. *Letters of Marque* were granted to two Bristol ships, the *Maryflower I* and *Seabright* in 1585.

John Whitson, a Bristol merchant was part owner of these ships. These ships secured two prizes laden with profitable goods, including sugar. Concerned that the ordinary seamen did not share in the bounty he distributed his share amongst them and also amongst the poor of Bristol. It is said that he sold his part share to a Thomas James and ceased all activities in privateering ventures. Whitson became Mayor of Bristol and represented the City in parliament. He is perhaps more well known for founding Red Maids School.

Not all those involved in privateering kept within their licence. In 1596 Captain Thomas Webb in command of the privateering vessel *Minion* attacked a Danzig ship, the *White Falcon*. Captain Webb was not licensed to interfere in the safe passage of ships from this region; therefore his attack on the *White Falcon* was an act of piracy. He stole the cargo and put the crew to the torture. He then proceeded to disable the captured vessel to such an extent that it foundered and sank with the loss of all hands. When news of this atrocity reached the authorities (the officers no doubt informed on by some of the members of the crew with a conscience) Captain Webb and those thought to have been complicit in the crime were arrested in Bristol and imprisoned. Unfortunately there does not appear to be an account of any trial, but we do know that the Mayor ordered the release of three of the prisoners. Captain Webb may have been related to Alderman Webb, who was later to become Mayor, so it was likely that there was no trial and the pirates got away with it.

During the period of the war Bristol fitted out a good number of ships for privateering ventures. These varied very much in size, from the 16 ton *Marline* to the 150 ton *Gift of God,* armed with 24 cannon. Other vessels licensed included the 80 ton *Bark Norton,* armed with 10 cannon and the *White Lion* of 60 tons. There is no doubt that the crews of these and other ships from Bristol were skilled seamen and very successful during the war.

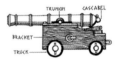

England was again involved with its many wars with Spain in 1625, a war which lasted for five years; it was the first year of the reign of Charles I. The usual *Letters of Marque* were granted in order to strengthen the force of King's ships. In 1627 England also became embroiled in a war with France. England could only take on two powerful countries like Spain and France because of her vast privateering fleet. Nonetheless there were reverses in Europe, but this was offset by the capture of Quebec, with the aid of a fleet of nine privateers fitted out in London. However, Quebec was returned to France in 1632. A significant change took place in the size of the vessels used by the Bristol privateers during the war.

They were larger than those used a generation before and more heavily gunned. The *Angel Gabriel* for example was a 280 ton ship and well armed; it was a formidable opponent. This was revealed when the Angel Gabriel came up against three Spanish ships and a fierce engagement took place. The Spanish ships were forced to flee with the loss of five hundred men. This may have been an exaggeration, particularly since the *Angel Gabriel's* captain reported a loss of only three of his own men. However, it does reveal the effectiveness of the larger ships and the ferocity of the Bristol privateers in close quarter fighting, as their vessel was boarded many times.

A Bristol built ship, the *Charles* launched in 1626 weighed in at 280 tons and carried 30 cannon. The *Bristol Merchant* was 250 tons and the *Adventure* 200 tons. There were, of course, smaller ships in use such as the *Bon Esperance* (90 tons) and the *Dove* (40 tons).

Examples of the varied range of goods seized by Bristol privateers were timber, tobacco, palm oil, cochineal, sugar and wheat. Another Bristol ship, the *Comfort,* captured a Spanish merchantman from Brazil carrying over 500 chests of sugar.

A ship of 70 tons, the *Henrietta Maria* was fitted out in Bristol and sailed from the port in search of the North West Passage. The vessel was commanded by Thomas James who became well known for his voyages of discovery. He failed to find the passage but made other discoveries and had many adventures. He published an account of these on his return, *Strange and Dangerous Voyage.* It is considered to be the source, or one of them, of Coleridge's *Rime of the Ancient Mariner.*

The Kirtlington Cup.
Presented to Captain Samuel Pitts by the Merchant Adventurers of the City of Bristol for bravely defending his ship 'Kirtlington Galley' 7th June 1628 against a Spanish Rover in his passage from Jamaica.

It must be said that Bristol profited greatly from this five year war. There were many prizes brought into Bristol laden with goods. The *Eagle* was particularly successful and one prize brought in carried a large cargo of sugar and hides. Her accompanying pinnace, the *Falcon* of 40 tons, brought in a further prize well laden with booty. At war's end it seems likely that many former privateers found it difficult to forgo the huge profits that were made during the conflict and a few probably resorted to piracy.

The First Dutch War of 1652-1654 was the first of three largely unnecessary conflicts between two Protestant nations. A shared tradition should have made them strong allies. Although there were many factors that were instrumental in the build up to war the chief cause was the growth of the two nations' maritime strength. Each saw the other as a threat. The first Dutch War took place at the start of the Commonwealth, the so called Interregnum. Cromwell (and others) introduced reforms to the navy and turned it into an efficient force. Consequently England did well in the conflict. The second and third Dutch Wars (1665-1667); (1672-1674) were not so successful. Charles II was restored to the throne in 1660 and the navy reforms under Cromwell ignored. During the second Dutch War the English were successful in the Americas, capturing New Amsterdam, and renaming it New York. Elsewhere, England found itself up against the Dutch, French and Danish fleets and forced to make terms. The navy reforms that had brought success during the first Dutch War were neglected again in the third Dutch War, which must also be considered unsuccessful. The war petered out when Parliament refused to grant further funds for the conflict.

It was fortunate that after the disastrous two Dutch Wars the lesson had been learned and the reforms introduced during the Interregnum were restored. These reforms became the foundation of what we know today as the Royal Navy, although it is interesting that they were first introduced during the time when England had no monarch.

Bristol's involvement in the second and third Dutch Wars was minimal, probably because privateers would have been at a disadvantage against a newly organized and dynamic Dutch fleet. In fact there appears to be no record of privateering ventures during the third Dutch War. Seventeen Bristol ships were licensed during the first Dutch War, a small number in relation to the numbers involved in other conflicts. This may of course have been due to the ravages of the recently ended Civil War. One of the licensed ships was the *Charles,* a 350 ton vessel carrying 20 cannon. Other ships were also heavily gunned for the period.

England was again at war in 1689, allied with Holland against France. This War of the Grand Alliance was lengthy and ended only with the *Treaty of Ryswick* in 1697. The element of this war in the Caribbean theatre is given in more detail in Part 1 of this narrative. It appears that *Letters of Marque* were granted to only eight ships during this war, a most unlikely number. The records may be incomplete of course, but those recorded were mainly large ships and would have been formidable adversaries to enemy merchant ships. The *Betty* was 400 tons and armed with 40 guns, quite capable of going up against a French warship. The *Bengal Merchant* was even heavier at 600 tons, also carrying 40 cannon. Another reason for the low number of Bristol privateers could have been the growing strength of the Royal Navy. Yet another reason could have been a steady supply of privateers from the English colonies, many of which had populations of third generation colonists with a vast knowledge of their local environment.

Five years after the *Treaty of Ryswick* England was engaged in another of her seemingly endless wars. The War of the Spanish Succession (1701-1713) was a war of complicated alliances. Matters came to a head in Europe following the death of Charles II, the last Spanish Hapsburg king in 1700. Agreement could not be reached as to how the Spanish dominions in Europe should be allocated. In 1701 the French captured Dutch fortresses in the Spanish Netherlands and occupied many ports. A treaty of Grand Alliance was agreed between the English, Dutch and the Holy Roman Empire. War broke out between France and Austria in Italy in 1702 and the new Grand Alliance declared war on France in the same year. Bavaria came in on the side of the Franco-Spanish alliance. Portugal entered the war on the side of the Grand Alliance and allowed the use of her naval bases for the English fleet, which was very active during the entire conflict. John Churchill (Duke of Marlborough) was the most successful commander during the war, but there were reverses as well as victories on both sides. Royal Navy and privateer units were active in American as well as European waters. England captured Gibraltar from the Spanish in 1704, starting that settlement's long association with this country. Nova Scotia on the American mainland was captured from the French by English troops, assisted by American colonists in 1710. This long war was ended by the *Treaty of Utrecht* in 1713 after prolonged negotiations.

Commander Damer Powell in his book *Bristol Privateers and Ships of War,* quoting two sources stated that only one action by Bristol privateers is reported in this war. The first source from Luttrel's *Brief Relation* (1678-1714), reveals that in July 1710...

two ships belonging to Bristol while on their way to the West Indies, were attacked by two French privateers of 110 and 90 men, that the British crews successfully defended themselves and actually captured their assailants, whom they triumphantly carried to Antigua.

The Bristol ships are not named. This lack of information is surprising as Bristol had an impressive array of privateers that were engaged in the Spanish War of Succession. As many as 128 privateers and *Letter of Marque* ships were fitted out in Bristol during this time. It is true that most of them were lightly manned, even the heavier ships armed with a large number of cannon. This would have made it nigh on impossible to fight the ships effectively, the crew having to divide their time between manning the cannon and manoeuvring the ships by sail work during an engagement. In addition to this a lightly manned vessel would find it difficult to repel boarders and in turn would find it equally difficult to board an enemy vessel. Some privateers however were well manned and carried sufficient crew to sail the ship and man the cannon. The *Duke*, a vessel of 300 tons and 30 cannon had a crew of 150 men; the *Duchess* also of 300 tons with 24 cannon, had a crew of 120. Ships such as these would have been capable of long voyages and would be quite capable of giving a good account of themselves against any French or Spanish ship they might encounter. The larger crew meant that the captain had the ability to board enemy ships with a reasonable chance of success. The wooden ships of the day were capable of surviving a huge amount of pounding from cannon shot. Having the facility to organize boarding parties was often the only way an engagement could be brought to a conclusion.

This lack of information concerning individual actions by the Bristol privateers makes one wonder if some of their activities might have been illegal, in other words they were engaged in piratical ventures. Whatever the truth of the matter, the Bristol privateers, together with their brethren from other ports and from the colonies must have been effective. French and Spanish trade was severely disrupted while British trade, although reduced, was not seriously affected.

The war however was to have a serious downside. Many privateers, having enjoyed long years of profitable enterprises were reluctant to forgo these profits. At war's end they became pirates, preying on ships of any nation. They became the scourge of the Caribbean and American mainland. This was the era of Blackbeard who had honed his skills of naviga-

tion and seamanship through long years of war. It took the Royal Navy several years to bring this pirate menace to an end.

In 1717 Britain, France and the United Provinces (Holland) formed a Triple Alliance to oversee the *Treaty of Utrecht*. This alliance was strengthened by the inclusion of the Holy Roman Empire in 1718. What became known as the War of the Quadruple Alliance broke out in the same year and lasted until January 1720. The purpose of the conflict was to force the Spanish out of Sardinia and return it to the Holy Roman Empire. The principal naval engagement was Admiral George Byng's victory over the Spanish fleet off Cape Passaro in August 1718. In January 1720 Spain joined the alliance and promised to settle territorial disputes by peaceful means.

Eleven Bristol ships or those fitted out in Bristol were granted *Letters of Marque* during this conflict. The heaviest privateer was the 250 ton *James* which carried 12 cannon and had a crew of 30 men. The heaviest gunned ship was the 170 ton *Cadogan* which carried 18 cannon; crew members are recorded as just 26. Crews in all eleven ships were still small in number, which, as stated earlier put them at a serious disadvantage when they came up against heavily armed and well manned warships. Still, they could be very effective as commerce raiders.

However, when the ships were properly manned

they could be quite formidable. Captain Johnson, in his book *The General History of Ye Pyrates,* written in the early eighteenth century, gives an account of such a happening, when in the absence of a Royal Navy man-of-war in the region of Barbados, two ships were commissioned to sail against the infamous pirate Captain Bartholomew Roberts. The pirate entered the West Indies in April 1720 and plundered a Bristol ship off the coast of Barbados. Captain Bartholomew Roberts let the ship, now empty of cargo, sail on to Barbados after a few days. Captain Johnson writes ….

being bound for the aforesaid island, she acquainted the Governor with what had happened, as soon as she arrived. Whereupon a Bristol galley that lay in the harbour, was ordered to be fitted out with all imaginable expedition, of 20 guns and 80 men, there being no man-of-war upon that station, and also a sloop of 10 guns and 40 men. The galley was commanded by one Captain Rogers of Bristol and the sloop by Captain Graves of that island, and Captain Rogers by a commission from the governor was appointed Commodore. The second day after Rogers sailed out of the harbour, he was discovered by Roberts, who knowing nothing of their design, gave them chase (assessing incorrectly that they were, as usual, undermanned for effectively fighting their ships). *The Barbados ships kept an easy sail till the pirates came up with them, and then Roberts gave them a gun expecting they would have immediately struck to his piratical flag, but instead thereof, he was forced to receive the first of a broadside, with three huzzas at the same time; so that an engagement ensued, and Roberts being badly put to it, was*

obliged to crowd all the sail the sloop would bear, to get off. The galley sailing pretty well, kept company for a long while, keeping a constant fire, which galled the pirate; however, at length by throwing over their guns and other heavy goods, and thereby lightening the vessel, they, with much ado, got clear; but Roberts could never endure a Barbados man afterwards, and when any ships belonging to that island fell in his way, he was more particularly severe to them than others.

The next conflict that heavily engaged privateers was the War of the Austrian Succession (1740-1748). Britain in fact had been at war with Spain from the previous year, but this was more to do with the indiscriminate attacks on British shipping. The War of the Austrian Succession was another war of complicated alliances but in reality was about the European powers trying to position themselves into the role of most powerful nation. British troops were committed on the continent, and were allied to the United Provinces. France joined the war against Britain in 1744. Hostile public reaction to Britain's involvement in the war was a factor that brought the war to a close in 1748.

Bristol privateers were very active in this war, with prizes being taken on both sides. It was a war of sharp and bloody exchanges and for the first time saw the Bristol privateers giving priority to the efficient manning of their ships. Prior to this war a complement of 200 men was rare, but it now became the norm. One of the reasons for this was that the privateers were likely to run into well manned and efficiently run warships whilst commerce raiding, either King's ships or heavily armed enemy privateers.

Privateers from other ports were often fitted out in Bristol, thereby bringing more revenue to the city. A major role of the privateer in 1745 was watching out for ships carrying supplies to aid the Jacobite cause in Scotland. It is reported that the *Trial* commanded by a Captain Conner intercepted and took the *Santa Zerrico* en route for Scotland. Another action of note was that of the *Sheerness* who took the *Fière* and the *Renard,* also in 1745. The *Sheerness* was a 450 ton ship, with 22 nine-pounders and 4 four-pounders. It was also armed with 12 swivel guns and crewed by 200 men of all trades. The Bristol privateer *Trial* had a previous success in 1744 when she single-handedly engaged five French ships of which three were captured. The 150 ton *Trial* carried 18 cannon and 12 swivel guns (an anti-personnel weapon). Such ships a few years before would have carried only 36 men but in 1744 a crew of around 100 was more usual. Another significant action by a Bristol ship was the *Alexander's* recapture of *HMS Solebay* from the French in 1746. This action was well reported at the time and Captain Phillips was presented to George II and received many honours. The *Alexander* was a 320 ton ship armed with 24 cannon and ideally would have been crewed with 250 men. At the time of her attack on the French-crewed *HMS Solebay* however the *Alexander* carried only 140 but was enough to do the job.

Another successful ship was the *Tiger* and she fought many courageous actions under the command of Captain Seix. The *Tiger* was a large ship of 560 tons and armed with 40 cannon and 6 swivel guns. Fully crewed she would have had a complement of 300 men. In 1748 the *Tiger* took the *Santa Theresa,* sailing from Havana, and brought her into Bristol. This was a good return for the owners as the prize was worth £40,000, a considerable sum in 1748.

The *Bristol* was launched in the city of that name in 1744. Only a year later she was unwisely or was tricked into engaging with the 64 gun *Elisabeth* who out-gunned her two to one. The first broadside severely damaged the *Bristol's* rigging and being unable to escape she was taken to Brest by the victorious *Elisabeth*.

The *Constantine* was a lucky ship. Of heavy tonnage but lightly armed and with a complement of only 40 men she could have been easy prey to Spanish and French warships. She bore a charmed life however and once managed to escape from a fleet of eleven French ships after a chase that lasted four hours. The very next day she encountered a lone merchantman, a rich prize carrying sugar and coffee worth £6,000. She towed the merchantman into the safe anchorage of the Downs off the coast of Kent. The *Constantine's* captain from the time of the French entry into the war was John Read and it was under his command that the most valuable prizes were taken. Many prizes were taken by the *Constantine* during 1747 but it was in 1748 that she excelled herself. On a voyage to Venice in January she encountered six French merchantmen and took three of them. These were the *Jean Baptiste,* the *St Blaize* and one other; they carried linen and silk. The prizes were taken to Malta and the *Constantine* carried on to Venice with her own cargo. The war ended in October 1748 which was probably fortunate for the crew of the *Constantine,* as it was doubtful if their luck would have held, given the extent of their risk taking. Although she survived the war her luck ran out when she sank off the coast of Jutland in 1752. However, some of her customary luck must have still been with her, as all the crew were saved.

The *Dolphin,* a small ship of 60 tons armed with 10 cannon and 12 swivel guns, was packed with 80 men. Commanded by Captain John Dyke, in July 1747 she took a brig and in July of the same year she took the French ship *St Joseph* and brought in this ship on her return to Bristol. The two ships were evenly matched in terms of fire power but it is doubtful if the small French ship had 80 men at their disposal to withstand a boarding party.

Receiving her *Letter of Marque* in August 1744 the *Dragon* commanded by Captain James Seaborn sailed in September. The 150 ton *Dragon,* armed with 20 cannon and twelve swivel guns carried a crew of 140; together with the swivel guns this made a formidable fighting unit. The *Dragon* captured the *Janeton Le Febevre* a 140 ton ship carrying fish from Nova Scotia. She also took the *St Aignan* and recaptured the *Severn,* returning her to England in 1745. Only one other prize is recorded as having been taken for the rest of the year, the *Fortune.* In May 1746, command of the ship fell to Captain Thomas Elworthy. A French ship, heavily laden with muni-

tions was taken by the *Dragon.* She also took a French privateer, no mean feat; together with a tobacco-laden brig. Another two prizes were taken before the *Dragon* returned to Bristol in November after a very lucrative cruise.

Bristol Privateers 'Boscowen' and 'Sheerness' fighting off eight French warships in 1745.

An incident on the 20th April 1745 demonstrates the handicap that a privateer faced when sailing with a reduced crew. The Bristol privateer *Dreadnought*, a ship of 300 tons and well armed with 20 cannon, carried a crew of only 50. It appears no swivel guns were mounted and in such a lightly crewed ship they were essential to prevent boarding. On the above mentioned day the *Dreadnought* was attacked by a French privateer, the *Grande Biche,* near St Malo and the Bristol privateer was boarded. They put up a stout resistance in the face of great odds. The crew carried on with their resistance even after their captain had been killed, but were forced to ask for quarter when a fire on board the *Dreadnought* spread to the gunroom. The life of a privateer was harder than it needed to be. They rarely co-operated with one another for mutual support and so put themselves at great risk, particularly in the Western Approaches where the French were not only active but numerous. It should be remembered that privateering ventures were just that, private ventures. A shared action meant a share of the prize and this the privateers baulked at.

The privateers were also demonstrating their legacy of the independent spirit of the buccaneer and seemed prepared to accept the risk in return for a large reward. However, when actions were organised by the Royal Navy, especially overseas, the privateers performed well, but they returned to their independent ways as soon as they were able. This made their use as an auxiliary force to the Royal Navy less important, even unreliable, as the eighteenth century progressed. In the war that followed the War of the Austrian Succession, the Seven Years War, the inability of the privateers to work together led to a serious disruption in British trade.

The above account of some of the actions undertaken by Bristol privateers in the War of the Austrian Succession is a snapshot only of their many and varied activities.

With the outbreak of the Seven Years War with France (1756-1763) *Letters of Marque* were again granted to Bristol ships. This conflict was significant for many reasons. Britain increased the extent of her new territories in the Americas and India; it proved that Britain's navy could hold its own against the two principal maritime powers of the day (France and Spain); it led the Admiralty into devising more effective ways of securing trade routes; blockades and convoys were more widely used and techniques developed that were in place by the outbreak of the long war with France in 1793 (the French Revolutionary and Napoleonic Wars).

There was, however, a negative side to this war that could not be seen at the time by Britain. It sowed the seeds for the loss of the thirteen colonies by the imposition of the Stamp Act of 1763, a way of raising revenue in America to help recover the costs of this most expensive war. The undemocratic nature of Britain's political system made her deaf to pleas of 'no taxation without representation', a cry not only heard from the American Colonies but in Britain as well. Although Britain emerged from the Seven Years War as the world's most powerful military nation, fear of this power by other European nations left her isolated and devoid of allies in the War of American Independence. By 1780 Britain was opposed by the French, Spanish and Dutch, all with powerful fleets; it was time for old scores to be settled. Faced with the real threat of invasion at home, fighting a major war on the American continent, having to defend its settlements in Canada, the Caribbean and India, only one conclusion was possible for Britain, the loss of the thirteen colonies.

On the outbreak of war in 1756 there was a clamour of activity to fit out as many ships as possible for privateering ventures. This first flush of enthusiasm led to the creation of the largest number of privateers ever furnished by Bristol. It was reported that this initial activity produced forty privateers for service in about a year. A further twenty ships were fitted out during the next two years. However, there appears to have been a drastic decline in the number of ships available for privateering ventures after 1758. As reported in *Felix Farley's Bristol Journal* of the 9th June 1759 ....

Of 56 privateers fitted out at this port there is at this time but a single one remaining at sea; the rest are either laid up or altering for mercantile service.

The declaration of war with Spain in 1762 led to a revival in privateering ventures, with several Bristol ships receiving *Letters of Marque*. This revival was of short duration however as the war ended on the 10th February 1763, the *Treaty of Paris* being signed on that date.

It seems an odd occurrence that such a vast number of privateers should be removed from the registers after the first three years of war. There was obviously more profit to be made in other forms of trade, perhaps even the slave trade, although as we shall see privateering ventures could be very lucrative if a cruise was successful. These profits however had to be weighed against the increasing costs of fighting an active fleet of French privateers defending their vulnerable merchantman. Far better to engage in trading ventures, evading the French privateers and fighting defensive actions only. This led to the Royal Navy having to divert its sometimes scarce resources to tackling the French privateers. In other words the privateers could no longer be relied upon to fulfil one of their traditional roles of acting as an auxiliary force to the King's navy.

In the early part of the war there were some notable successes by Bristol privateers, including that of the *Tiger*, a ship that had seen service in the War of the Austrian Succession. In 1756 the *Tiger* took the *Nestor* and the *Comte de Noailles*, but herself was taken by a French man-of-war in 1758.

The first Bristol privateer to be registered in this war was the *Anson*. Fitted out in Sea Mills Dock in 1756 she was commanded by Captain Wapshutt who had a reputation of being a hard, even cruel commander. She left on a short voyage on July 2nd 1756 and returned in August with two prizes, the *Marie Esther* of 500 tons and the *Aimiable Julie* of 160 tons. The prizes were worth £20,000. Together with the *Constantine*, in June 1758 she took another ship bound for a French settlement in the Americas. Some time later, together with the *Dreadnought* (in a rare combined privateering venture) she took a French privateer, the *Bayonetter* together with a prize the privateer had taken, the *Anna*.

In 1758 the Bristol ship *Bellona* was involved in an operation that reveals how privateers should have ideally been used. In April of that year the *Bellona*, a ship of 110 tons and armed with 16 cannon and 10 swivel guns, was cruising off Rochelle. A report in *Felix Farley's Bristol Journal* dated May 27th 1758 states that the Bellona, commanded by Captain Richards went into St Martin's Port, near Rochelle on April 26th 1758 and ....

cut out 14 French merchantmen, two of which, of 100 tons, each laden with wine and brandy, he has brought into Galway. The other twelve the captain hopes have got safely into other ports in Great Britain or Ireland. This action was done at noon within gunshot of seven French men-of-war of the line and four frigates. The captain supposes these to be part of the fleet dispersed by Admiral Hawke.

This refers to the fleet action by the Royal Navy against French ships of the line, frigates and transports, loaded with troops and stores en-route for America; many of these transports were beached. A marine action on the Isle d'Aix destroyed the facilities there, the force being extracted safely. The remnants of the French fleet, although still powerful, were likely to have been distracted and unsettled by their defeat, which allowed the *Bellona* to operate effectively in French waters. *Felix Farley's Bristol Journal* further states that ....

Swivel gun in action

Hawke sailed on the 6th, having effectually prevented the dispatch of supplies to America, and, it may be, so facilitated the conquest of Cape Breton and its dependencies.

There is little doubt that the *Bellona* and her prize crews had assisted in the final endeavour by their capture of the fourteen merchantmen.

The following is a list of some other Bristol privateers and their exploits during the early years of the Seven Years War.

The *Enterprize* was a ship of 200 tons, armed with 20 cannon and 10 swivel guns. She carried a crew of 150 men. After receiving her *Letter of Marque* in April 1757 she sailed from Bristol under the command of Captain Nicholas Lewis. In that year she captured a large French ship, the *Amphion*. In November of the same year she took a brigantine. In 1758 the *Enterprize* was patrolling in the Mediterranean and in February captured a ship which she ransomed. In March the *St Joseph* was taken. She took five more prizes before being taken herself and ended up in Toulon.

The *Ferret* sailed from Bristol in June 1757 and by July had captured two prizes. After taking them to Falmouth (which suggests that the action took place in the Western Approaches) The *Ferret* resumed her cruise. She brought another prize into Bristol in October. The *Ferret* was a small ship of 70 tons but was well armed with 10 cannon and 8 swivel guns and carried enough crew to fight the ship.

Another well manned ship, the *Fortune,* the former prize *Esperance,* sailed from Bristol on July 4th 1757, commanded by Captain John Emerson. Although only of 100 tons the *Fortune* carried 14 cannon and 6 swivel guns and was manned by a crew of 100. As we have seen, ships that carried a full complement of men were not only more likely to be successful in their ventures but also had more chance of returning safely from a voyage. Of course there was still the chance that they could come up against a warship or a privateer that out-gunned them but by and large the well manned ship would have a better chance of survival. The *Fortune* falls into this category, for on her first voyage she had amassed seventeen prizes in three months.

The *Jason,* commanded by Captain Thomas Gibson captured four sloops in October 1758 and took them into Antigua. In May 1760, but this time commanded by Captain John M'Greagor, the *Jason* was captured herself and taken into Marseilles. This is not surprising as although of 200 tons with 16 cannon she had a complement of only 45 men. A *Letter of Marque* ship, the *Jones* was taken in May 1760. Of 200 tons and carrying 14 cannon she had a crew of only 40, a small number considering she traded as a slave ship. The *Jones* was sailing in the West Indies when she was taken.

The *John and Elizabeth,* whilst voyaging from Bristol to Tortola had the misfortune to fall in with a French Privateer. The *John and Elizabeth* fought a fierce engagement with the privateer despite having a crew of only 16 men. She was finally taken and ended up in Martinique.

Another *Letter of Marque* ship, the *Marlborough* suffered an engagement similar to the one experienced by the *John and Elizabeth.* In February 1760 the *Marlborough,* under the command of Captain Samuel Richardson arrived in Jamaica with 252 slaves. It is reported that a few days before her arrival the *Marlborough* had been intercepted by a privateer of 14 cannon and 150 men; the Bristol ship however was equal in strength to the privateer. She was armed with 16 cannon and 10 swivel guns and carried a crew of 120 men. The privateer suffered much damage and withdrew from the action, although three of the *Marlborough's* crew were killed, including Captain Richardson. It is not reported if any slaves had been killed.

This trading voyage of the *Marlborough* reminds us that the slave trade was still very active in Bristol. It was to be nearly thirty years before Thomas Clarkson first came to Bristol to gather evidence that was eventually to lead to its abolition. He took lodgings at *The Seven Stars* public house in Thomas Lane, where he was befriended by landlord Thompson, who knew of his mission. Thomas Clarkson also visited the other slaving ports of London and Liverpool (where he survived an assassination attempt).*

The *Tartar* sailed from Bristol in 1756 and had a successful first voyage as a privateer. In November of that year she took the *Cadiz Packet,* a former British ship captured by the French. The *Tartar* also captured the *Elizabeth* and the *Joseph Olive.* On January 19th 1757 she captured the *Sally,* another prize of the French. In May 1757 the *Tartar* took on

*See *Cry Freedom, Cry Seven Stars,* by Mark Steeds.

a French privateer, the *Vin du Village* and captured her. Such a ship as the *Tartar* could engage not only merchantmen but ships designed for combat. The *Tartar* was of 200 tons, carried 22 cannons and was well manned, having a crew of 100. During the above mentioned exploits the ship was under the command of Captain John Shaw.

As stated earlier, Britain's declaration of war on Spain in 1762 led to a brief revival of privateering ventures by Bristol ship owners. However, the Seven Years War was concluded in the following year so the revival was of short duration.

In 1762 thirty three ships fitted out in Bristol were declared as having *Letters of Marque*. Of these only twelve had seen service as privateers before, the *Ann, King David, Levant, Minehead, New Grace, Oldbury*, Planter, Ruby, Sally, True Britain, True Patriot* and the *Young William.* Of the thirty three ships fitted out in Bristol only two, the *Levant* and *New Grace* were sufficiently manned, and there is a question mark over the *New Grace.* It appears likely that captains and ship owners had difficulty in recruiting seamen for privateering ventures, particularly now that Britain was at war with Spain, as well as France. War's end saw Britain in a very powerful position and her neighbours wary of her.

Chain Shot

*Later lost off the West Coast of Africa with hundreds of slaves on board

Twelve years after the end of the Seven Years War Britain was involved in another conflict that found her assailed on all sides. Initially, Britain's war aim was to suppress rebellion in the thirteen colonies, but the French, Spanish and Dutch took advantage of the situation and the American War of Independence became a global conflict for Britain.

This war was entirely avoidable, the root cause being Britain's reluctance to consider the introduction of democratic principles into government. A simple extension of the franchise, both in Britain and America would probably have been enough to prevent the conflict. Independence could then have been achieved by peaceful means some time in the future.

There certainly was a case for independence and Tom Paine, a Norfolk man, made a statement to this effect in his published work *Common Sense,* which sold in vast quantities in America. However, the British Government was in no mood to listen. In fact the move into a form of democratic government was long and laborious and it was to be over 150 years before all citizens, irrespective of gender, had the right to vote.

The War of American Independence is generally reckoned to have commenced when British and American forces came into conflict with each other at Lexington and Concord in April 1775. However, there had been skirmishes before this date.

To the alarm of Britain the French declared war on her in 1778, followed by Spain a year later. The

Dutch followed suit in 1780. A series of indecisive fleet actions left Britain without complete control of the sea and facing the threat of invasion at home. With her naval forces split and conducting a major continental war Britain's resources became over-stretched and she had to take stock.

In February 1782 a motion was approved in the British parliament that there would be no further attempt to subdue the thirteen colonies by force. On April 12th 1782 a decisive victory over the French fleet in the Battle of the Saintes by the Royal Navy secured control of the sea in the West Indies for Britain.

This caused some consternation to the American colonists as despite the recent assurance by Britain that she would make no more attempts to subdue them by force, that was before Britain had regained control of the sea. The Americans feared that there was a possibility that the British would launch a full scale invasion. But Britain really was taking stock of her situation. Despite the odds she had success-fully defended her territories in Canada from the American colonists; she had also successfully defended her settlements in the West Indies and India and secured Gibraltar from the Spanish. Peace negotiations opened with the Americans in November 1782 and later with the other combatants. The *Peace of Versailles* was signed by all parties in September 1783.

Another contributory factor in the drive for peace, although a minor one, was that opposition politicians openly sympathised with the American cause, as did reform minded dissenters who had long doubted the justice of the British position.

Numerous privateers fitted out in Bristol took part in this war, but not very successfully. Substantial loss-es were experienced by ship owners. It is recorded that only one prize was taken of any note, the *Ferne* captured by the *Alexander* and *Tartar* and brought into Bristol in 1778. This is not strictly true as other valuable prizes were taken by Bristol privateers, but they did not match the value of the *Ferne*. However, what is true is that many Bristol ships were taken and overall the American war was littered with loss mak-ing ventures.

The most successful Bristol privateer was Captain John Shaw who had seen active service in the War of the Austrian Succession, the Seven Years War as well as the American War. He died on December 20th 1796 and was buried in Shirehampton church-yard. A monument was erected there that bears the following sentiment ….

Sacred to the memory of John Shaw Haven Master of Hungroad Port of Bristol and Formerly Captain of the 'Lion' Privateer of 44 guns and 168 men which on the night of the 6th of December 1778 engaged 'L'Orient' French Man of War of 74 guns and 800 men, the scene of the Action was the Bay of Biscay where after 2 hours close engagement the enemy was beaten off with the loss of 137 killed and 244 wound-ed, the 'Lion' had 22 killed and 19 wounded, this gallant commander died December 20, 1796, Aged 80 years.)

Monument to Captain John Shaw in Shirehampton Churchyard. A photograph probably taken in the late 1920s. The monument is now totally covered in Ivy.

The following is an account of some of the actions of Bristol privateers considered successful by their owners.

The *Alert* was a well armed 100 ton ship. It carried 16 cannon and was crewed by 35 men. In June 1781, the *Alert* commanded by Captain William Llewellyn arrived in Bristol following an African cruise. The *Alert* had taken three Dutch prizes during this cruise and secured 1,000 ounces of gold-dust and 10 tons of ivory from one ship before releasing her. One of the other ships was a slaver with over 300 slaves on board and was sold locally, presumably together with the slaves, a shameful transaction. The remaining ship, the *Aurora* came into Bristol in August 1781 with a prize crew.

The 200 ton *Albion,* armed with 16 cannon with a complement of 50 men had several successful cruises during the American War. She sailed from Bristol in September 1778 under the command of Captain John Gardner, and returned with two prizes, the *Robuste* and the *Minerve.* Both ships were sold in Bristol. On her next cruise, together with the *Tartar,* she took the *Santa Maria,* a ship formerly taken herself as a prize. This ship was taken into Kingroad (off Portishead).

In March 1781 the *Albion* herself was taken by the French ship, the *Madame* but was retaken in October of that year. In late 1782 the *Albion,* by this time commanded by Captain John Everitt, together with the *Hector* captured the *Virgin del Carmen.*

The *Byron,* in 1779, together with a Liverpool privateer the *Friendship* captured a French ship trading between South Carolina and France. She carried a mixed cargo of tobacco, indigo and rice. The *Byron* had another success a little later when she took the American privateer *Yorick.* In 1780 the *Byron* took a large American ship and sent her to Barbados. The *Byron* was a ship of 250 tons and had 20 cannon, but the key to her success was surely the twelve swivel guns she had mounted and the large crew of 150 men. She would have been an intimidating sight in a close quarter engagement.

A small ship, the *George,* of 95 tons was nonetheless crewed by 70 men and armed with a 16 cannon mix of six and four pounders. In January 1779, under the command of Captain Peter Wade, the *George* captured the *Effingham* carrying a cargo of masts. She returned to Bristol in April of that year. The *George* sailed again from Bristol, this time commanded by Captain John Major in June 1779 and took the *San*

Jeronimo, described as carrying wine and bale goods. The *San Jeronimo* was sent into Cookhaven at first but later arrived in Bristol and sold. In May 1781 the *George* was lost to a gale, but it was reported that the crew were saved.

The *Hornet* was heavily armed with the newest weapon of the day, the carronade. This was a short-barrelled gun that fired a very heavy shot and was devastating at close range. It was quickly named the *Smasher* by its users. The *Hornet* had 22 of these and in addition had 10 twelve pounders. A full complement of 180 men crewed the ship which made her

A Carronade. This weapon fired a 68lb shot.

a formidable opponent. The *Hornet* was of 350 tons. Captain John Kimber was in command of the *Hornet* when it took the *Defence* carrying a cargo of tobacco. The *Defence* was sent to Bristol in 1780 and sold. In the early part of 1781 the *Hornet* took part in a fleet action that succeeded in capturing Dutch colonies in Surinam.

In April of that year the *Hornet,* together with the *Surprise, Revenge* and *HMS Surprise* (that carried the same name as the privateer she was in company

with) took the Dutch ship *Three Friends.*

In January 1782, the *Hornet* still under the command of Captain Kimber took a total of five prizes, including the Spanish ship *Purissima Conception* which was considered a very rich prize. It is not surprising that the heavily armed and well manned *Hornet* made such a valuable contribution to the war effort. The *Hornet* was reported as being wrecked in 1794 but the crew were saved.

Another successful Bristol ship was the 296 ton *Jupiter.* As a privateer she took twelve prizes, some of which were brought back to Bristol and sold.

As will be seen from the above brief account of Bristol privateering ventures, the most successful ships were those that were adequately manned or combined their operations. There appears to have been no overall plan by the owners to combine their resources. They could have sent out fewer ships but adequately crewed, or sent ships out in company.

Bristol privateer 'Ranger' with prizes taken in the American War.

The Bristol privateer 'Caeser' hove to.

Ten years after the end of the American War another conflict broke out between the European powers. This war, known as the Napoleonic War (for ease of description) commenced in 1793 and finally ended with the defeat of Napoleon at Waterloo in 1815.

Although Bristol privateers had been active in preceding conflicts their activity in the Napoleonic War was minimal. Very few ships were fitted out specifically for privateering ventures, although *Letters of Marque* were granted to some other trading vessels. It seems that because of the substantial losses incurred by ship owners in the American War they were adopting a once bitten, twice shy policy. Other reasons could have been the slow decline in Bristol's position as a major port, a series of business and bank failures and priority being given to what we would call today speculative building. Quite simply, it was not worth the risk to invest in privateering. Ship owners preferred their trading vessels to sail under the protection of convoys, a facility that was becoming more common. There were still however fast, well-armed and well-manned ships called runners or running vessels that were permitted to sail on their own. Runners were usually granted *Letters of Marque*.

Although there were a few examples of owners co-operating, any combined operations were likely to have taken place due to the initiative of individual captains. Being a privateer must have been a risky venture during this war, bearing in mind that Britain was opposed by French, Spanish and Dutch ships and an active American privateering fleet. As the war advanced the Royal Navy relied more heavily on convoys as a way of protecting shipping and some privateers were engaged in escort duties. In this role the Bristol privateer *Caesar* did valuable service. The *Peace of Versailles* brought an end to all hostilities between Britain, France, Spain, Holland and the new American republic.

Probably the first prize of the war taken by a Bristol privateer was the Swedish ship the *Freden* in May 1793. The privateer was the 63 ton *Bess*. After a temporary peace in 1801, ratified by the *Treaty of Amiens* in March 1803, hostilities resumed in May 1803. A Bristol privateer, the 234 ton *Eliza* armed with 14 cannon was in action in July of that year. She captured a Spanish vessel and a French ship the

Princess Royal. Both ships were sent into Kingroad. In August 1803 the *Eliza* captured the *Gloire,* a French ship of 400 tons and this was also brought into Kingroad. In October of the same year the *Eliza* brought another ship into Kingroad, the American *Young Eagle,* who was trying to run the blockade. In November 1803 the *Eliza* was put up for sale, after a short but successful privateering venture. Perhaps the owners did not want to push their luck. Having made a good profit and still holding on to their ship they obviously though it was prudent to put the ship up for sale rather than risk another cruise. As if to demonstrate that there was little appetite for privateering in Bristol the *Eliza* was still unsold in February 1804, under terms of 'any reasonable offer considered'.

According to Commander Damer Powell's research which he has included in his book *Bristol Privateers and Ships of War,* the last recorded prize taken by a Bristol private ship of war was an American vessel in the summer of 1812. The Bristol ship was the *Sir Alexander Ball,* a 20 cannon ship of 410 tons. In 1814 the *Sir Alexander Ball* was intercepted by the heavily armed and well-manned American privateer *General Armstrong.* The Bristol ship had no more than 40 men, an inadequate number. An account in *Felix Farleys Bristol Journal* of July 16th 1814, reads ….

"'Sir Alexander Ball', Captain Skynner, on passage to Malta, was attacked in 39°45 N, 10°39 W, 80 miles from Lisbon, by the 'General Armstrong', American privateer, and after a severe action of twenty minutes was taken. The American was con- *siderably heavier in metal and better manned. The 'Sir Alexander Ball' had six wounded, of whom two are not expected to recover. The crew were taken to Lisbon and the prize sent to America. The latter was retaken on her passage across by 'HMS Nieman', and arrived at Halifax on 20th July."*

There was an extensive ship building programme in Bristol during the Napoleonic War, with the shipyards busy constructing merchant ships and ships for the Royal Navy.

One of the major lessons learnt from the Seven Years War and the American War was that the Admiralty could not rely on privateers to effectively disrupt an enemy's trade. British commerce was savaged by French, Spanish, Dutch and American privateers. The British privateers forgot their role as an auxiliary force to the Royal Navy. For example, they failed to work together by blockading ports and coordinating small fleet actions. In this they were displaying the independent spirit of the traditional buccaneer. It was this unreliability of the privateers in the Seven Years War that gradually led the Royal Navy to rely less and less on their services. Although ships from Bristol and the Channel Islands were particularly active during this conflict and built up an impressive record of prizes it was felt that an expansion of the Royal Navy was a more effective way of providing security for the country.

By the start of the French Revolutionary and Napoleonic Wars the Royal Navy was in a position to develop its strength to a point when at war's end Britain became the world's principal maritime power. It was even powerful enough to engage the United States in the War of 1812 whilst conducting a major European campaign. Britain used sea power to bring the Anglo-American War to an end. With the peace of 1814 in Europe the Royal Navy was able to reinforce its units off the United States coastline. The Royal Navy locked up the American Navy in their bases and severely disrupted American commerce. This led directly to the *Treaty of Ghent* in December 1814 which brought the war to an end. It took five years for American overseas trade to recover from the Royal Navy blockade.

Although privateers continued to operate throughout the Napoleonic War their contribution to the war effort was minimal. Not that their ventures were without risk; they operated in isolation and in hostile waters. The end of the war was the beginning of the end for the privateers. In 1856 Britain signed an agreement *(Peace of Paris)* formally ending its involvement in privateering. There was however a 'left over' from privateering days. The Royal Navy had a long tradition of prize courts, a department of the Admiralty that ruled on the value of ships or property taken by naval vessels. The prize courts also decided on the share each crew member should receive. Many captains of frigate commerce raiders became rich on account of this system. Prize courts were still operating years after the 1856 agreement.

During the nineteenth century and well into the twentieth century Britain's navy became a powerful force. It enabled the country to punch well above its weight and to influence world events, even to imposing its will on other countries. Whether or not this use of maritime power was always wisely or justly used, is a matter for debate.

Can any lessons to be learned by an examination of the history of buccaneers and sea rovers? I believe so.

As we have seen, the Spanish encroachment into the Caribbean and the Americas and the way they conducted themselves had a devastating effect on the inhabitants of the entire region. This led to the gradual expansion of empires on a global scale, the effects of which we are still experiencing today. These empires have been replaced by a new imperialism taking the form of a rabid free market and neo-liberalism. State and corporate piracy is often the first cause of many of the world's disasters, from global warming to endless wars. How different it may have been if the words of Bartolomeo da Las Casas had been heeded and the expansion into the New World had been replaced with fair and just trade.Las Casas gave sensitive and good advice that was ignored by those in power. In a sense, Las Casas in his moving human rights speech of 1550 was making an appeal for an appreciation of other peoples' cultures, to be aware of the uniqueness and joy in diversity and to resist the imposing of one culture on another, this out of respect for our shared humanity. Las Casas came to the understanding that all humankind is one by a combination of logic, reason and faith. Four hundred and fifty nine years later Dr.

Alice Roberts of Bristol University in the BBC series *The Incredible Human Journey* was able to present evidence that proved that we are all out of Africa, that all humankind is indeed one and that we all share our future as well as our past. In my view a recognition of this would be the establishment of a system of global fair trade to replace the aggressive competitiveness which is a feature of the free market. At the very least we should make an attempt at this, otherwise we are little better than the buccaneers and sea rovers that many years ago roamed the Caribbean in search of plunder.

Ken Griffiths.

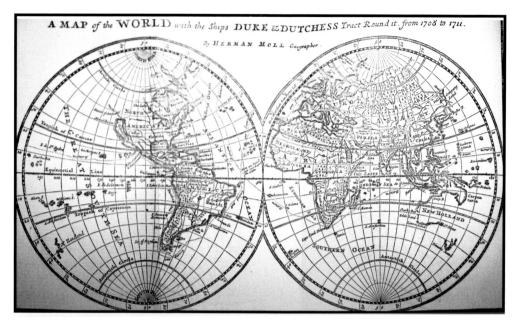

The 1708 - 1711 map of the world showing the voyage of the 'Duke' and 'Duchess' comes from the frontispiece of Woodes Rogers' famous book 'A Cruising Voyage Round the World'.

THE JOLLY ROGER

The French privateer Du Casse was fond of hoisting a red flag to indicate 'no quarter given' and it was with this in mind that pirates and buccaneers developed their own flags. The buccaneers and pirates realised the effectiveness of this terror tactic and quickly adapted flags of their own.

They embellished red and black flags and used iconography prevalent in this period - the skull, skeletons and various body parts, combining them with other symbols pertinent to their chosen occupation; swords, spears, daggers and even the occasional hour glass indicating time is running out for the intended victims.

These symbols of death and destruction were taken up by several 18th and 19th century British regiments, the 'Death or Glory Boys' who utilised this form of intent to great effect. As late as the 20th century the iconography was used again by various organisations such as the Nazi SS to intimidate their chosen victims.

This 17th century symbol comes from a tomb in St Mary Redcliffe Church that lies between Canynge's and Penn's tombs.

Appendix 1

The centre of this new emergence of piracy is Somalia. The root cause of the problem is the breakdown of law and order in that country. A barely functioning government presides over a condition of political and social instability with no way of protecting it's citizens; poverty and anarchy is the result. The economy of Somalia has been further depressed by the deployment of commercial fishing fleets from developed countries in or near Somalian waters. Technical fishing aids on these ships puts Somalian fishermen at a disadvantage and must be considered as unfair competition, particularly bearing in mind the plight of the Somalian people. Without an effective government to protect them the result is piracy.

It seems that in the long term the best way to prevent the activities of the Somalian pirates is to encourage the Somalian people to work towards forming a functioning government. Economic and humanitarian aid, without strings, would be a useful tool in helping to achieve this. In the meantime ships and sailors must be protected. This can probably be best achieved by using the age old, tried and tested method of ship protection, the convoy system. Far better that this system should be used rather than employing the services of military contractors (mercenaries) as is being suggested. The use of contractors would work against any long term solution. In a sense the deployment of mercenaries would be a return to the buccaneering era, with all its attendant problems.

Appendix 2

The 1670 *Treaty of America* between England and Spain heralded a significant shift in the politics of the region. Although both countries would be in conflict again it was the first serious attempt to secure peace in the West Indies. One of the advantages to England of the treaty was the freeing up of resources to counteract the growing territorial ambitions of France, ambitions that much later were to explode into full scale war in North America. Both England and France were ambitious rivals, vying for domination of the region. Nonetheless, the *Treaty of America* was also an attempt to limit the power and activities of the buccaneers. The following is a list of some of the most important Articles of the Treaty.

Article II. *There shall be universal peace and sincere friendship, as well in America as in other parts, between the kings of Great Britain and Spain, their heirs and successors, their kingdoms, plantations etc.*

Article III. *That all hostilities, depredations etc, shall cease between the subjects of the said kings.*

Article IV. *The two kings shall take care that their subjects forbear all acts of hostility, and shall call in all commissions, letter of marque and reprisals, and punish all offenders, obliging them to make reparation.* (this was the section of the treaty invoked to bring the buccaneers into line).

Article VII. *All past injuries on both sides shall be buried in oblivion.*

Article VIII. *The king of Great Britain shall hold and enjoy all the lands, countries, etc. he is now possessed of in America.*

Article IX. *The subjects on each side shall forbear trading or sailing to any places whatsoever under the dominion of the other without particular licence.*

Article XIV. *Particular offences shall be repaired in the common course, and no reprisals made unless justice be denied or unreasonably retarded.*

Appendix 3.

The distinction between a privateer and a *Letter of Marque* ship was sometimes very slight, but the main practical difference was that the privateer was usually more heavily armed and manned. The privateer was privately owned and crewed and granted a government commission *(Letters of Marque)* that authorised it to be used against an enemy nation, usually in the seizure of merchant vessels; it was specifically fitted out for that purpose. Privateers were also used as an auxiliary force to the Royal Navy. In this capacity they were employed in fleet actions, combined operations and in the protection of convoys, particularly during the Seven Years War (1756-1763) and the American War (1775 - 1783).

A *Letter of Marque* ship was a merchantman whose specific task was trade. If however they came across an enemy merchantman they were permitted to take it as a prize. They were basically opportunists but could cause havoc with enemy shipping if successful. Sometimes of course they became victims themselves, but if captured the crews were protected by the *Letters of Marque* from being tried as pirates.

Bibliography

Ashton, John: *Chapbooks of the Eighteenth Century.* Chatto and Windus, London, 1882.

Bayley, Christopher (Editor): *Atlas of the British Empire.* The Hamlyn Publishing Group Ltd, Amazon 1989.

Betty, J.H.: *Bristol Observed.* Redcliffe Press, Bristol, 1986.

Braybrooke, Lord Richard: *The Concise Pepys.* Audley End, 1825. (1988 edition by Wordsworth Editions).

Burney, James: *History of the Buccaneers of America.* First published in 1816, Swan Sonnenschein & Co., London, 1891 edition used.

Breverton, Terry: *Black Bart Roberts.* Wales Books (Glyndwr Publishing) Vale of Glamorgan, 2004.

Brown, Harold G.: *Bristol, England.* Rankin Bros. Ltd. 1946.

Cawthorne, Nigel: *A History of Pirates.* Arcturus Publishing Ltd. (Capella imprint), London, 2003.

Cordingly, David: *Pirates – An illustrated history of priva-teers, buccaneers, and pirates from the sixteenth century to the present.* Salamander Books Ltd., London, 1996.

Coleridge, Samuel Taylor: *The Rime of the Ancient Mariner.* Joseph Cottle, Bristol, 1798.

Craton, Michael: *A History of the Bahamas.* (3rd Edition) San Salvador Press, 1986.

Damer Powell, J.W.: *Bristol Privateers and Ships of War.* J.W.Arrowsmith Ltd., Bristol, 1930.

Dampier, William: *A New Voyage Round the World.* London, 1697.

Darvill, P.A. and Stirling, W.R.: *The Expanding Years.* Schofield and Elmo Ltd., Huddersfield, 1973.

Defoe, Daniel: *Robinson Crusoe.* London, 1719.

Earle, Peter: *The Pirate Wars.* Methuen, London, 2003.

Evans, John: *A Chronological Outline of the History of Bristol, and the Strangers Guide Through its Streets and Neighbourhoods.* Published by the Author, Bristol, 1824.

Gardiner, Juliet and Wenborn, Neil (Editors): *The History Today Companion to British History.* Collins and Brown Ltd., London, 1995.

Griffiths, Ken and Gallop, Roy (illustrator): *Highway Robbery, A Brief Look at Highwaymen and Highwaywomen.* Fiducia Press, Bristol, 2007.

Hakylut, Richard: *Voyages and Discoveries.* Late 16th Century (1985 edition by Penguin Classics used, with an introduction by Jack Beeching).

Hardy, Robert: *Longbow.* Patrick Stephens Ltd., Sparkford, Somerset, 1976 (1992 edition used).

Hazlewood, Nick: *The Queen's Slave Trader.* Harper Collins

Publishers, New York, 2005.

Hudleston, Roy C.: *How To See Bristol*. J.W.Arrowsmith Ltd, Bristol, 1931.

Hutton, Stanley: *Bristol and its Famous Associations.* J.W.Arrowsmith, Bristol, 1907.

Johnson, Captain: *General History of Ye Pyrates.* London, 1724 (various editions used).

Jones, Donald: *Captain Woodes Rogers' Voyage Round the World.* Bristol Branch of the Historic Association, 1992.

Kurlansky, Mark: *Cod.* Jonathan Cape, London, 1998.

Manwaring, G.E.: *Woodes Rogers – Privateer and Governor.* Cassell and Co. Ltd., London, 1928.

Marley, David F.: *Pirates: Adventurers of the High Seas.* Arms and Armour Press, 1995.

Marley, David F.: *Pirates and Privateers of the Americas.* ABC-CLIO inc.,Santa Barbara 1994.

Nicholls, J.F. and Taylor, John: *Bristol Past and Present Volumes II and III.* J.W.Arrowsmith, Bristol, 1882.

Norris, Gerald: *The Buccaneer Explorer – William Dampier's Voyages.* The Boydell Press, Woodbridge, 2008.

Novak, Maximillian E.: *Daniel Defoe – Master of Fictions.* Oxford University Press, 2001.

Paine, Thomas: *Common Sense,* First published in 1776. From *Rights of Man, Common Sense and other Political Writings.* Introduction and notes by Mark Philip. Oxford University Press, 1998.

Pilger, John: *Hidden Agendas.* Vintage, London, 1998.

Preston, Antony: *History of the Royal Navy.* Bison Books, London, 1983.

Preston, Diane and Michael: *A Pirate of Exquisite Mind.* Doubleday, London, 2004.

Robinson, Derek: *A Shocking History of Bristol.* Abson Books, Abson, Bristol, 1973 and 1987.

Rogers, Woodes: *A Cruising Voyage Round the World.* London, 1712.

Souhami, Diana: *Selkirk's Island.* Weidenfield and Nicholson, London, 2001.

Steeds, Mark: *Cry Freedom, Cry Seven Stars.* Bristol Radical History Group, Bristol, 2008.

Stevenson, Robert Louis: *Treasure Island.* Cassell and Company, London, 1883 (1999 edition by Penguin Classics used, with an introduction by John Seelye – The official book of Bristol's Great Reading Adventure, 2003).

Swift, Jonathon: *Gulliver's Travels.* London, 1726.

Trustees, Long John Silver Trust: *The Bristol Treasure Island Trail.* Broadcast Books, Bristol, 2005.

Williams, William: *The Journal of Llewellin Penrose – a Seaman.* John Murray, Bristol, 1815.

Wood, Michael: *Conquistadors.* BBC Worldwide Ltd., London, 2000.

Zacks, Richard: *The Pirate Hunter.* Headline Book Publishing (Review imprint), London, 2003.

Papers: -

Dewhurst, Kenneth and Doublet, Rex: *Medical History.* Notes on pages 107-121 of Vol. 18, 1974 "Thomas Dover and the South Sea Company".

Lewis, Huw and Quarm, Roger: *The Mariner's Mirror.* Notes on pages 345-350 of Vol. 93 No.3 August 2007 "The Journal of Llewellin Penrose" – A new acquisition for the National Maritime Museum.

Acknowledgements

Sources of illustrations, engravings, photographs and maps.

Lhc: left hand column. Rhc: right hand column.

Engravings from Woodcuts by *Thomas Bewick and his School:* Pages 6, 25, 28, 30, 51, 104 and 105 lhc.

Engraving from 18th century chap book: page 47.

The Century Magazine, vol. 23, 1882: pages 105 rhc and 112.

Ambrose Cowley: page 27 (map).

Roy Gallop: pages 1, 3, 9 (map), 10 (map), 13, 14 rhc, 24, 26, 31, 33, 36, 42, 46, 55, 60, 61, 66, 71 lhc, 71 rhc (top), 72 rhc, 76 (bottom), 78 rhc, 86, 87 (bottom), 88, 89, 90, 91, 94, 96, 98, 101 lhc, 102 (bottom) and 106 (bottom).

Photographs by Carol Griffiths: pages 7, 17 and 19. Colour centre fold photo of Admiral Blake stained glass window.

Engravings from Captain Johnson's *Ye General History of ye Pyrates:* pages 63 (bottom), 67, 71 rhc (bottom), 72 lhc, 73, 75, 76 lhc (top), 78 lhc, 79, 83 and 84.

Frank Shipsides: page 2.

Engravings and illustrations from Mark Steeds private collection: pages 14 lhc, 34, 37 and 63 lhc (top).

Photographs by Rosie Tomlinson: page 12. Colour centre fold photographs of the tomb of William Canynge, Richard Hakluyt memorial plaque, Admiral Penn's memorial, The 'Robinson Crusoe' Candlesticks, the Martin Pring memorial and the plaque to Thomas Clarkson.

Photographs by Rosie Tomlinson taken at the Bristol Record Office Archive: pages, 4, 38, 39, 43, 49, 85, 87, 93, 100, 101 rhc and 102 lhc.
Photographs by Rosie Tomlinson taken at the Bristol Central Reference Library: pages 48, 53, 57, 59, 77 and 106.

Worcester Cathedral: colour centre fold image of Saint Wulfstan.

Photograph from the LJS Trust's collection: page 111.

Our thanks to….

Dawn Dyer and her colleagues of the Bristol Central Reference Library.

Richard Burley and his colleagues of the Bristol Record Office.

Pat Terry, parish administrator of St Mary Redcliffe Church.

The Diocesan staff of Bristol Cathedral and St Stephen's Church.

The Bristol Radical History Group.

Royston Griffey and his colleagues on the *Matthew.*

Tess Green for her advice and guidance.

Dr.Ihasn H. Mian and his colleagues at Glenside Hospital Museum, Bristol.

Bristol Industrial Archaeological Society.

Long John Silver Trust

"Scratch an Englishmen and reveal a pirate" – as the author of *Shogun* and *Tai-Pan,* James Clavell, liked to relate in his best selling novels, and the saying is probably even more true for Bristolians, who have enjoyed many a high seas adventure as we have seen.

Little wonder then that Robert Louis Stevenson launched *Treasure Island,* his magnificent tale of greed and skulduggery in the city that started a thousand ventures, Bristol – home to perhaps more pirates and privateers than anywhere else in the British Isles. A book of world renown, *Treasure Island* features Bristol as it should be portrayed, with its safe haven the backdrop for ancient hostelries and traders, vibrant with cultures from around the globe, an image lost today with the damage inflicted by the Luftwaffe, post war planners and with the gentrification of the docks.

Over decades campaigners have asked for a sculpture of Long John Silver, one of Stevenson's most finely drawn characters, who personified a theme that RLS would come back to time and again - that of duplicity. A force for good one moment and bad the next, running with the hare and the hounds, trying to survive and thrive.

It has been said that Silver's inner conflict matches that of Bristol itself where the spectre of slavery casts a long shadow over everything. But it also begs the question of what drove him - was he a privateer discarded in time of peace, transported for stealing a loaf of bread or merely on the wrong side in a conflict? Any city in

Frank Shipsides launches the LJS Trust with Mike Fussell outside the Hole in the Wall with a ghostly 'Silver' looking on.

the world would be delighted to have such a famous fictional character as Silver to call their own and the Long John Silver Trust has been set up to try and make this happen.

The Trust didn't want to be a drain on the public purse and so decided to become a Registered Charity and with the remit of being educational and inclusive. This has spawned the Bristol Treasure Island Trail, with the potential of taking people from Bristol's most historic street, King Street, to the Museum of Bristol on Wapping Wharf. Just like *Treasure Island* the Trust started with a map, uniquely telling the story in a sequence of seven locations around Queen Square, Redcliffe and Spike Island.

Marrying it with real people and events from Bristol's past, we believe the old docks would once again spring into life with the characters that made it happen. Who could deny that in Stevenson's chapter on the *Captains Papers,* where Dr Livesey, Squire Trelawney and Cap'n Smollett plotted their voyage, it could just as easily have been Dr Thomas Dover, Pilot William Dampier and Cap'n Woodes Rogers doing the same thing on Welsh Back in 1708?

The Trust has some great people on board with Patrons Royston Griffey; a former Lord Mayor of Bristol, Sebastian Peake; whose father Mervyn created some of the finest ever illustrations for *Treasure Island* and Nicholas Newton; whose father Robert portrayed Silver on the big screen in a version that has never been topped.

Why not join us as well?
Please go to
www.longjohnsilvertrust.co.uk

Fiducia Press is a non-profit making community publisher specialising in local and social history, transport and poetry. For a full book list contact the address below or the Bristol Book Publishers shop website.

www.bristolbooksandpublishers.co.uk.

An Old Buccaneer.

This book is published by Fiducia Press, 10 Fairfield Road, Bristol, BS3 1LG.
The design and contents are copyright and may not be reproduced in any form without written permission of the publishers.